Thanx for!

Happy Sunsets,

"A laugh-out loud, make-you-cry, piss-you-off, stand-up-and-cheer book from an exciting new voice coming out of Key West"—**Jon Breakfield, author of the KEY WEST series**

"Life is what happens when you're making other plans"—**John Lennon**

About the Author

Born and raised in Chicago, Illinois. After serving as a radioman in the Navy (*USS Edward McDonnell*, De-1043), Will studied art and design at Southern Illinois University in Carbondale, Ill. He then toured as a sculptor on the Art and Renaissance Fair circuits for 7 years.

In 1976, calling on his experience as a high school gymnast, Soto re-invented himself as a physical performer. Upon moving to Key West, he started as a juggler and eventually progressed to funambulist (wire/rope-walker).

Will has performed extensively across North America, Europe and the Caribbean for more than 40 years, receiving major media (video and print) coverage in hundreds of national and international markets.

Will Soto is one of the original founders (1984) of the Key West Cultural Preservation Society, Inc., which is the managing non-profit corporation of the Key West Sunset Celebration Festival. His image on the high-wire, with the sunset behind him, has become the iconic image of the internationally renowned nightly event.

Will is the founder/director of BUSKERFEST, Key West's International Festival of

Street Performers, as well as a martial artist (Taekwondo Black Belt), and a backcountry kayak guide.

At 73 years of age, Will has finally slowed down enough to write this, his first book.

He and his wife Amy, along with their four dogs and a cat, live and love in the Florida Keys…and, yes, when he's not traveling for festivals and conventions, you can still see him performing at Sunset at Mallory Square in Key West.

QUOTES

"It matters not
The job you've got
As long as you do it well.
Things are made by plans well-laid;
The tests of time will tell.
But how can you count
Or know the amount
Or the value of a man?
By the show displayed,
Or the beauty made
By the touch of the juggler's hand"
—Robert Armstrong Nelson III. aka Butterfly Man

"Do not go where the path may lead. Go instead where there is no path and leave a trail"**—Ralph Waldo Emerson**

"The greatest glory in living is not in never falling, but on rising every time we fall"**—Nelson Mandela**

"You know you are on the road to success
if you would do your job and not be paid for it"
—Oprah Winfrey

"Time is nature's way of keeping everything from

happening at once"—**Jon Archibald Wheeler**

"All you need in this life is a tremendous sex drive and a great ego. Brains don't mean a shit"
—**Capt. Tony Tarracino**.

Key West Rogue Diaries

by

Will Soto

KW
Press

Key West Rogue Diaries

copyright © 2020

This book is dedicated to:

Amy Meshew-Soto

Will and Elaine Soto

Captain Tony Tarracino

TABLE OF CONTENTS

FORWARD

Once Upon a Time on a Small Tropical Island...

My first visit to Key West was hardly memorable. I was a radioman on a US Naval destroyer escort (*USS Edward McDonnell* De-1043) that port-of-called here in 1966-1967. Actually I don't remember much about it. Not that it wasn't interesting or fun... it's just that I was drunk all the time. A sailor in uniform is almost always served alcohol and, being a teenager, it was more of a temptation than I could bear.

I did, however, remember that the place had a funky kind of charm that was almost frontier-like.

After the service, and followed by college (Southern Ill. University), I spent 7 years as a sculptor working the Art Fair/Gallery circuit throughout the South and Midwest. Then one February, after working at the Coconut Grove Art Festival in South Florida, I ran into an old friend of mine, Dennis Blankenheim, who invited me to come down and visit with him in Key West. "Maybe just for the week-end," I said. "I'm really anxious to get back to New Orleans." So off we went, crossing the

42 bridges of the Florida Keys. It was late when we arrived so we just drank some home-coming rum and hit the sack.

The next morning I woke at sunrise to the smell of gardenias. It was February and it was sunny and warm. I couldn't get outside fast enough. As I walked down the lanes of Old Town I was overwhelmed by how many flowers were blooming, and how sweet the air was. Coconut palms, hibiscus, bougainvillea and frangipani everywhere. It was, and still is, intoxicating. I was smitten, and bitten (more or less against my will).

That was 1976 and it was my second visit to Key West. Honestly, like so many others, I only intended to stay a few days. It's now 2020 and I've begun my 44th year in Key West and the Florida Keys… and, holy moly, have I got a few stories for you.

I'll do my best to remember what I can through the haze of the drug and sexual revolutions. I am also guilty of plying my "Old Timer" friends with cafe con leche and liquor (and worse) to get them to help me remember/resurrect the characters, the escapades and the sheer joyful lunacy of living on an island that is "**Close to Perfect**, yet **Far from Normal**." (The Tourist Development slogan.)

CHAPTER #1

Cayo Hueso

In order to fully appreciate the mosaic which is Key West, I'll begin with my own personal observations seasoned with the history of a town that was once a base for pirate operations.

The name KEY WEST is originally derived from the name *CAYO HUESO*, which loosely translates to Bone Island. Legend has it that early Spanish and Bahamian settlers discovered numerous bones thought possibly to be from an earlier indigenous Indian battle. Through time and language changes, the name eventually morphed into KEY WEST.

This tiny island (1 x 3 miles) dangles at the end of the 100-mile chain of keys stretching WSW from South Florida. It also borders the Florida Straits which are the entrance to the Gulf of Mexico.

During the Civil War, when the rest of Florida sided with the Confederacy, Key West's Ft. Zachary Taylor was held by the Union. It was proven that whoever controlled the Florida Straits controlled all access to the Gulf of Mexico (Mobile, New Orleans, Galveston) and parts of the Caribbean. In the early 1800s it was that exact dynamic that made the Keys' many islands and channels a perfect haven for pirates. Famous pirates like Blackbeard and Capt. Kidd used these hideouts to ambush cargo ships in the nearby shipping lanes. It wasn't until 1823 that the US Navy sent Commodore Matthew Perry to combat the piracy and, ultimately, establish Key West as a Union and navy town for the foreseeable future.

Key West is a town that has experienced many boom & bust phases through the years. Some of those booms had been the mid-1800's wrecking industry, when Key West was the richest city per capita in the country, and others were the sponging industry, turtling, the cigar industry, and the shrimping industry. When I arrived in 1976 it was obvious the 70s were not a boom. The Navy had recently closed their port of operations which caused the economy to tank. Half of Duval Street, the main street of Old Town, was boarded up. If it wasn't the tropics, one could've expected to see tumbleweeds rolling down the lanes. Shopkeepers were quick to put up their GONE FISHING signs in the steamy, hot afternoons. Phone numbers had only 5 digits and calls only cost a nickel. But it wasn't exactly a bust either. It was as if the town was taking a rest and pondering how to reinvent itself yet again. The bridges to the mainland were being rebuilt in the 1980s and the roads were getting repaved, so TOURISM was the obvious and logical suspect to be the next boom. In 1976 it was still quiet though, with the Pier House and the Southernmost Hotel being the only guest accommodations on lower Duval Street. It was in this introspective era that the nightly tradition of **Sunset Celebration** was quietly born, and its manger was a weathered and aging commercial dock named Mallory Pier.

The *Green Flash,* the optical phenomena that sometimes occurs at the exact moment of sunset, was obviously its conception.

.

CHAPTER #2

PARADISE is where your realities are more exciting than your fantasies

The Key West fire that burns in my soul didn't start as a conflagration.

It started as a nice warm sun on my face—and it started at **Mallory Square.** Imagine stumbling upon a beach party on a small tropical island, with barely clad natives, their bodies glistening with sweat, dancing to primal drum beats, smoking ritual herbs, and drinking rum from coconuts as the sun sank slowly into the ocean. It sounds like a steamy novel, but I swear it's all true, except that the beach party was taking place on a concrete pier.

Within the first day of arriving in Key West in the mid-70s, I found my way down to Mallory Square, where I discovered the nightly ritual known only as "**Sunset.**" I'd heard it was a place where people would go to watch the sun go down and commune with their neighbors. An hour or so before the sun sank on the west side of Old Town, locals would trickle down to this old crumbling commercial dock which was about 400 feet long and only 20 feet wide. Folks would gravitate to the water's edge, say a few hellos, grab a seat where they could dangle their legs over the crystal-blue water and enjoy whatever they had brought to drink. Here was a small, wonderfully exciting mix of the entire socio-economic spectrum. Young and old, natty or gnarly, workers, slackers and dreamers, all just gathered at the water's edge to say "Goodbye" to the sun and "Hello" to the evening. They all had this serene look on their faces that silently screamed "I've found Paradise!" Indeed they had, but they weren't about to tell anyone. Among those sun worshippers was generally an itinerant musician or two who would serenade both the sun and the small crowd. Occasionally a traveling juggling show or magician would pop in and, street style, add some fun to the mix. The colorful food vendors were pretty much out of a Carl Hiaasen novel.

The *Cookie Lady* (Marilyn Kellner} sang rhymes... "Key West sweets, Key West treats. Buy one and we both can eat!"

The *Conch Salad Man* (Frank Baing) sang songs about how conch salad made you horny. The nightly event was a veritable cauldron of eccentricity. It was a scene worthy of Federico Fellini.

The mood was so serene it almost seemed to be in slow motion. Maybe it was the warm, moist tropical breeze, or maybe time just passed at a different pace there, but the results were both sedate and seductive. The magic in the air was palpable. It hung over everything much like the hot, blanket of humidity that permeated life here. Locals had a coined saying that I've always loved: **"Key West is not the end of the world...but you can see it from here."**

There were locals and travelers, artists and fishermen, hippies and divers, smugglers, troubadours and entrepreneurs. Most people appeared to be an intriguing combination of several of these. A fierce individualism was their common thread; that, and a wonderfully low-stress laissez-faire attitude that reflected the identity of the island. People cared more about your attitude than your profession. It was generally understood in those days that you didn't ask people's last names or what they did for a living. It was as if **Low-Key** had married the **Wild West** and they had a baby named **KEY WEST**.

CHAPTER #3

HOME is where the HEART is

A popular saying in Key West is that once you get Keys' sand in your sandals, you are destined to return. Now in my fifth decade of living here, it's obvious that it's worked on me. Growing up in Chicago gave me my Midwestern roots and demeanor. Living in New Orleans stimulated my cultural growth. It wasn't until I lived in Key West that I blossomed as an individual.

Things that I only had dreamed about until then suddenly became, not only possible, but probable. This book is dedicated to the magic, the people and the environment that shaped most of my adult life. Some of these stories may actually look like fiction, but that is exactly what life has been like living here. Here are but a few of them. I hope you enjoy reading them as much as I've enjoyed living them. Not all the stories occur in Key West, but they all have their roots in my Key West soul and inspiration.

* * *

It was winter in Key West when I arrived in February of 1976, if you could call 80 degrees winter. I actually slept on the beach for about a week while I decided if I was staying. That really sounds romantic and exciting until you wake up in the hot Florida sun getting bitten by things you can't see.

If I were going to stay, I needed housing. No problem. There were more weathered old conch houses for rent than there were old weathered conchs, a nickname for the locals. In those days, if a house in the historic Old Town district was renovated, it stood out like a sore thumb among the old sun-bleached shipbuilders' homes. (Nowadays a house that's NOT renovated stands out.) It didn't take long to find a funky two-story wood frame conch house that reportedly once belonged to artist and poet Henry Faulkner, a close friend and companion of Tennessee Williams. Kentucky-born and considered an eccentric Bohemian, Faulkner was best known for his vividly colorful paintings and wild art-show parties where he would bring his bourbon-drinking goat, named Alice. Perfect. I shared the house, 328 Peacon Lane, (formerly named Grunt Bone Alley) with fellow sun setter and new friend O.J. Dave Del Rosso. Dave was the ultimate tie-dyed hippie and, 43 years later, he still is (and that's a good thing).

Where to begin?

How about a new profession?

I came to the Keys as a traveling sculptor. I exhibited my sculptures at galleries and several Renaissance Faires. It was there that I began to hang with the performers a little more than the artists. I always sensed, intuitively, that they were having more fun than anyone else. I always enjoyed practicing juggling, etc., with them and they always teased me about being a "closet" performer.

Having a background/hobby in gymnastics and juggling, I was inspired by the many busking shows (street performing) I had seen at these faires and in my travels. Two creative personalities who GREATLY influenced my evolution into performance art were the classic clown Avner (The Eccentric) Eisenberg, best known for starring in *The Jewel of the Nile*, and legendary juggler Turk Pipkin, author, comedian, pianist and film director. My eternal thanks for the inspiration both of these gentlemen provided me.

The Sunset Celebration at Mallory Square would be the perfect place for my metamorphism. It was at this gathering that I first summoned the courage to attempt performing in public. Putting yourself out there in front of a crowd can be incredibly intimidating but the warmth of the people there made me feel they might laugh WITH me instead of AT me. Thank God I was right. It was 1976 and I was no longer Will the sculptor. I was now Will the Juggler. I still remember riding my bike home after my first week of performing and thinking *I love this. I should've tried this years ago.*

I can't deny that there were a few bumps (and bruises) on the road. It's true that at 30 years of age I was changing my profession to be a busking juggler. Most of my friends actually told me to go sober up, but my parents, true to their supportive selves, said "Go for it. Life's too short not to do what you want." Thanks Will & Elaine. You're the BEST.

Performing as a "**Busker**" meant passing your hat after the show's finale and accepting whatever the crowd was moved to donate. My favorite part was that it didn't have to be money, although that fed me and paid the rent ($50 per week in 1976). Leaving it to the crowd's imagination turned into "Christmas every day." Besides the usual monetary rewards were surprises, delights and treats befitting a visiting dignitary. To name a few there was home-cooked food, hand-sewn clothing and home-made jewelry, massages, historical artifacts, joints, plane tickets, theater tickets, thousands of new friends/dates, three wives, a son and, finally, a soul-mate. I had also found both myself and a new home.

Sometime in the early 80s I visited a fellow Busker named Bounce (Margil) the Clown. He, and his performing wife/partner Mademoiselle Ooh-La-La, also lived in Key West. He was one of my inspirations in the "circus arts". He was also one of the very first juggling shows to busk at Sunset Celebration (circa 1975).

Bounce had a practice tight wire set up in his backyard that was just a few feet off the ground. The gymnast in me teased me to try it. Oh My God. It felt so…natural. I felt as if I'd been doing this my whole life. As I look back, I realize this was my Eureka moment. The fickle-finger-of-fate had poked me right in the spirit. I knew immediately that I wanted, and needed, to learn more about

Funambulism, the art of rope walking. I can never repay Bounce enough for inspiring and encouraging me to take that first step. To this day, even though he's younger than me, I still look up to him.

I borrowed some rope and went to Bayview Park. I picked out a couple of buttonwood trees and tied my line about two-to-three feet off the ground. The formula is the same as juggling. You just KEEP practicing until you quit dropping or falling. The hours turn into days, and then months turn into years. It soon became more than just a matter of balance though. It was now becoming pure Zen. It was a tacit realization that when I was out on the rope or wire, it was a place where only I could go. It was peaceful and safe and there was no one there but me. I had discovered my spiritual spot in the universe.

Before long I began performing on the tightrope and high-wire and my new transformation was complete. Festivals that I used to work at as an artist were now hiring me as a performer. The New Orleans Jazz & Heritage Festival was the first to believe in me and trust me to go high. It was only about 22 feet between two oak trees, but it was a start. Their production crew (Hometown Productions) foreman, Tague Richardson, gave me the support I needed to think bigger. He would always ask me "What can we do to help you?" Indeed, he had the heavy equipment and know-how to make things happen. "You want us to sink some telephone poles or build a tower?" Through the years working with them I eventually walked across water hazards blindfolded and across a pit filled with live alligators. Thanks Tague. This was getting to be more fun and stimulating by the year. Eventually I graduated to walking between the tops of buildings, and the rest is history. It's never been lost on me that all this magic started when I arrived in Key West. The truth is, at least for me, the magic's never ended.

CHAPTER #4

Unclear and Present Danger

Not long after settling into my newly adopted home, I discovered kayaking. It's not a stretch to imagine that boating in the Keys, surrounded by the Atlantic Ocean and Florida Bay (Gulf of Mexico), is an idyllic pastime. Add to that the hundreds of small mangrove islands that dot the shallow Keys' waters and you have an inviting and picturesque tropical paradise just waiting to be explored. I couldn't wait.

I called Pete Lazzaro, an old Chicago friend who had also just relocated to the Keys and said "Let's go on a kayak adventure." I had heard of a small island called Indian Key that had a colorful past.

As the story goes, a local Key West wrecker named John Housman had a falling out with other Keys' wreckers and decided (or was forced) to relocate. It just so happened that there was a small uninhabited Key just offshore, oceanside, about 80 miles north, which had a deep-water approach from the East. A deep-water port being essential to salvage operations, Mr. Housman decided to move his entire operation, work crew, family and worldly belongings to Indian Key to start a new life. It was the early nineteenth century and wrecking on the Florida reefs was extremely profitable. The uncharted and treacherous waters of the near-shore reef provided an endless supply of shipwrecks. According to Maritime law, the first salvor to affix a line to a sinking vessel and rescue the crew could then claim ownership of all the cargo. Ships continued to run up on the reef, and business was so good some of Houseman's other relatives came to live and work with him. He built himself a comfortable home and one for his crew. Eventually he built a structure that housed a general store, post office and two-room hotel. Life was so good that he applied for a charter to become the Seat of Dade County, and was accepted. Fate had smiled generously on Mr. Housman...except for one thing.

The neighboring island was inhabited by a local Indian community (rumored to be Seminoles). They also claimed sovereignty over John Houseman's new settlement. After watching the Housman clan settle and develop land they believed to be theirs, they had finally had enough. On Aug 7th, 1840, the Indians boarded canoes, crossed the shallows and raided the white settlement. They burned down the entire community and killed many of its inhabitants (rumor has it that Housman's wife and daughter survived by hiding in a cistern). To this day you can still see the foundations, cisterns and dirt roads that were once a small village.

My curiosity (and love of history) was calling me. Pete and I loaded up my tandem kayak on my old Toyota truck and off we went to launch at Mile Marker 78. The kayak was hot, the air was hot, and the water was hot. Thankfully it was only a mile or so to the island. As we paddled out, I told Pete the whole story. This was great. It was just the adventure we were looking for (more about Pete later in this book).

We beached on the windward side and walked a bit to identify any of the ruins that were still visible. Other than a few birds, it was a virtual ghost town/island. It was eerily quiet from the lack of buzzing mosquitos due to there being no fresh water on the 12-acre island. The Housmans had sourced their fresh water from nearby Lignumvitae Key. I'm sure the task of retrieving said water was a welcome trade-off for the absence of those pesky tropical blood-suckers.

Happy as a couple of stoner explorers could be, we decided to sit on some rocks near the shore and break out the flask of rum and a joint that we'd brought. Sipping Cuban rum and smoking Jamaican ganja with our toes in the water.

Pete smiled, "Does it get any better than this?" We were thrilled, blissed and stoned at the same time when suddenly we heard it.

It sounded like gunfire off in the distance across the island. We froze. The gunfire was getting closer. We stared at each other with a mix of curiosity and dread. Then we heard voices, and they didn't sound happy. Not knowing exactly what to do we retreated to the tree line. The gunfire got louder. We hid behind a small cluster of Australian Pines, trying to see but not be seen. By this time we were trying to figure out if we could creep back to our kayak and paddle silently away. Then I saw them.

Coming around the tip of the island were two canoes full of Indians, in full regalia, firing muskets and yelling. If I didn't admit that I almost wet my pants, I'd be lying. Pete and I looked at each other silently for a second, sweat dripping off our noses, and then busted out laughing.

We had unwittingly strayed into a historical re-enactment. Unfortunately, we had already thrown away our rum and weed, but the story will stay with us forever. It's the kind of tale that makes life here a constant joy, surprise and adventure (if you don't mind wetting your pants once in a while).

CHAPTER #5

Timing is Everything

As you will see, some of my stories are humorous, some are inspirational and some are just plain terrifying. This one is a tribute to timing and fate.

Once upon a time, I was a licensed Physical Trainer. When it was time to renew my license I had to take the Red Cross life-saving refresher course. Having taken it several times before, I was slightly bored but the instructor made it entertaining so I was along for the ride.

When it came time to practice the Heimlich maneuver on the rubber dummy we all made the usual jokes and took our turns hugging the doll-in-distress.

Two days later, I'm at Mallory Square doing my show. There's a nice crowd and I'm having fun joking with them. Just as I'm finishing a juggling trick, I see someone in my peripheral vision going down on one knee. A middle-aged gentleman's suntan had begun to turn blue. I stopped and focused on him. He appeared to be choking. The woman next to him grabbed him and said "I'm a nurse. Let me see if I can help him". Turns out her arms were too short to get any leverage on him. My mind raced to our CPR Red Cross instructor.

I ran over, grabbed the tourist and spun him around. He was pretty much like putty now with no resistance. I got a good bear hug on him and gave it my best shot. NOTHING. As I was taught, I tried it again. STILL NOTHING. After no response on the third try, he was passing out and I was SERIOUSLY concerned. Since he was pretty much dead weight by now I had to literally lift him up and bounce him to try it again. POW!!! A ball of dough, from a hot dog he'd been eating, suddenly shot out of him like a champagne cork. (Turns out the lifting action, instead of squeezing, was what did the trick.)

Anyway, I helped him to where he could sit, got him some water, and went on to finish my show to a bewildered crowd that couldn't figure out if it was part of the show.

After the show I looked for him but he was nowhere to be found. My mind returned to my instructor and how fateful it was that I was just re-learning that technique. I also felt that I had forged an incredible bond between the tourist and myself, yet he was gone. Oh well, the end result was so satisfying that I was pumped for days.

Two weeks later I get a call from someone who says "Hi. You don't know me, but I'm business partners with a gentleman named Bob Cole. You saved his life while he was choking. I told him that I was coming to Key West for vacation and he asked me to deliver something to you. Can you meet my wife and me at our guest house?"

"Sure," I said, and scooped up my own wife, Amy, and we headed over to the Palms Guest House. When we got there the gentleman handed me a bag. In it were a box and a card. The card had a lovely thank you note with a phone number that he requested I call. When I called, Bob answered and said "Wait a sec," and held the phone out so I could hear his two kids shout "Thanks for saving our dad!" He then apologized for having left as quickly as he needed a shower and some rest before his 7am flight home. "Open the box," he said, and I did.

Inside was a gorgeous Citizen solar-powered ECO watch. He said "Timing is everything. Thanks for being there for me."

That was over ten years ago but it's proved to be a great gift that keeps on giving, because now Bob and I are great friends and I know his entire wonderful family, from his mom to his kids and grandkids. We have even vacationed in the Everglades together. What greater gift is there than friendship.

And, yes, I think of Bob every time I look down to see the time.

It's everything.

CHAPTER #6

Changes in Latitudes, Changes in Attitudes

An interesting part of performing at festivals and special events is that each one is a different setting, a different occasion and a different clientele. In my 40-plus years of performing nationally and internationally, I have also appeared in shows at hundreds of Florida Keys tiki-bars, hotel conventions, and tropical parties with Jimmy Buffett music, piña coladas, and partiers in flip-flops.

One memory that continues to give me a chuckle was a beach convention party at an exclusive enclave in the Upper Keys. This particular luxury resort catered primarily to the upper crust. But then, everyone's equal when we're all in flip-flops, right? Well, sort of.

I had just arrived mid-afternoon to begin setting up my equipment for a soiree on the beach at sunset. As I was "loading in," I walked past the clubhouse, carrying some of my gear.

Out of the clubhouse come three giggling ladies. White hair, flowing white summer dresses, bejeweled sunglasses and sandals with rhinestones. I guessed mid-70s and from Palm Beach. As they passed me, one of them stopped and asked me: "Do you work here?" I told them, yes, that I would be performing on the beach at the sunset party. She stopped to catch her breath, looked around, and said "Well, we just heard a rumor in the ladies' room!"

I said, "Well, c'mon, now you have to tell me what it is."

She beckoned me closer and whispered conspiratorially: "We hear Buffett's going to be here tonight!"

Well, since Jimmy Buffett is practically synonymous with the Keys and I knew him from his beginnings on Mallory Square, I thought I'd thrill her by saying "Oh, Jimmy? He's a good friend of mine from the old days."

She just looked blankly at me and said, "No... *Warren* Buffett."

"The times they are a-changin'"—B. Dylan

CHAPTER #7

Time Flies Like an Arrow

Upon switching my profession from sculpting to performing, I definitely noticed the recognition that came with entertaining in public.

The more I traveled and appeared at festivals, events and marketplaces, the more I was being approached, by name, by strangers. This has always proved to be a valuable asset.

As any traveler will tell you, meeting people on the street is your first taste of their culture...and their first taste of yours. Not only each country, but each city, town and community has its own distinct flavor and idiosyncrasies.

A particular favorite of mine is Switzerland. Although a majestically beautiful Alpine country, I had often heard it referred to as "extremely conservative," whatever that means. For that reason I wasn't surprised when I was detained and interrogated by the local police for street-performing in Zurich, Switzerland's largest city. The police were stern but polite. Once they ascertained that my juggling knives were no threat, they released me with no charges, and a suggestion to move on. No problem. It was the early 80s and I was sleeping in the back of a hatchback car I had leased for the season, so traveling was my passion anyway.

It became quickly evident to me that the smaller the town, the friendlier and the more hospitable people were. Although that seemed to be a universal trait, it was even more so in Switzerland. As I street-performed in Lucerne, Basel and Bern, folks did more than tip me with currency. They made me feel comfortable. They invited me to their homes. They cooked me meals, and they offered me housing. They treated me as an honored guest and a visiting theater star. This was more like it. I stayed longer than I had intended and made far more friends than I expected. Switzerland, a mostly snow-capped country, made me feel warm and comfortable and I've never forgotten that.

Forward 25 years to Mallory Square in Key West, Florida, on a perfect Chamber-of-Commerce evening. As I was preparing to start a show at the Sunset Celebration, two stunningly gorgeous young ladies walked up to wait for the performance. I mean they were so hot that I forgot what I was doing. Their Daisy-Duke shorts and remnants of tattered t-shirts were suddenly making me feel like a young buck again. We exchanged flirtatious glances and I felt my pulse pick up. I'm guessing they were in their mid-20s and I detected an accent. *Be still my beating heart.* They smiled and giggled and I was suddenly pumping testosterone like a stallion. I was ready.

They were ready, and the crowd was primed. I started out with some fire-manipulation, a few mildly inappropriate jokes and built up to juggling knives on the tight-rope.

Glistening with sweat, I finished with a flourish and the crowd roared. As the happy gathering began to break up, I glanced sideways to the major babes and they were positively chirping. Sensing a familiarity, I said "Where are you ladies from?"

"We are from Switzerland!" they happily tittered.

"That's awesome," I gushed. "I had the most wonderful time performing in Switzerland. Bern was my favorite. The locals there took such good care of me".

"Awesome!" they echoed. "We are from Bern! Too bad we didn't get the chance to see you there."

Eternal *Wise-Guy* that I am, I backed up, looked them up and down with a smile, and said: "Well that was many years ago. I could actually be...your dad."

Without missing a beat, one of them backed up a little and looked ME up and down, and dryly said "Grandpa."

(Yes, it left a scar)

CHAPTER #8

Salt Life

Seeing that Key West is an island that's 100 miles to sea, it's only natural that many of my adult life-altering experiences were oceanic.

As a child, I grew up inland and always cherished fishing with my family. Everyone went. My mom and dad, siblings, and sometimes my grandpa. We would all pile into our family sedan, a gray 1954 Hudson, with a trunk full of tackle boxes and a cooler full of baloney sandwiches and Kool-Aid. The fishing poles, as a sign of the times, stuck prominently out the back side windows. It was definitely a clan thing. It was in those pre-air conditioned days, when we drove with most of the windows open just to get a 92-degree breeze.

We lived for those angling vacations and week-end camping outings. We went up north Oshkosh, Wisconsin, for pike, and out west to Jackson Hole, Wyoming, for trout, caught perch and salmon in the Great Lakes, and catfish in the Missouri Ozarks. But we lived in the heartland, Illinois, so most all the fishing we did was in fresh water.

When I came to Key West it was like going to a new planet for me. Growing up in the Midwest, Mother Earth was the dominant spirit and the lakes and rivers were the arteries incidental to the landscape. Historically, early travel and commerce moved most efficiently by boat via waterways.

In the Florida Keys, it's the opposite. Mother Ocean is sovereign and the skinny chain of islands, called keys, is the only way to get to sea in a car. You are literally living at sea. In the islands they call it *Salt Life*.

In Key West, a whole new world opened up to me. There was world-class fishing offshore and in the shallow flats. You could cast for sandwich sized snappers inshore, and luau sized mahi-mahi or trophy sized marlin out deep past the reef. I was always amazed (and still am) that when we went deep-sea trolling, the bait we used was as big as the fish we actually caught inland. It was a different challenge altogether. When you're offshore, every time your pole signals "FISH ON!!!" you might be in for a battle with a marine mammoth. It easily could be bigger than you. When you suddenly get strapped into a fighting-chair, you quickly realize why it got the name. And, at the end of an epic and exhausting battle, you could bring home one fish that will feed your whole neighborhood. In landlubber terms, that would be the difference between hunting rabbits and hunting elk.

But that's only the beginning. On the surface there was sailing, as close to flight as you can get without leaving the earth. On windless days there are hundreds of mangrove islands and shallow waterways to discover. You can kayak silently in water as clear as glass over coral heads and schools of literally thousands of uniquely colored fish.

Underwater there was snorkeling, Scuba diving and spearfishing at the reef and on dozens of wreck sites. Considering all the options, the Florida Keys have definitely earned their bona fides as a water-world paradise.

This *Salt Life* story is about sailing, sort of. It's also about survival. I've heard a coined phrase that describes sailing (and piloting aircraft) as "long periods of bliss and boredom, punctuated by moments of sheer terror."

It all started when my friend, Bucky Montgomery said, "Hey, I'm selling my sailboat. Know anyone that's interested?"

It was a cute little 22-foot Hunter that needed some love and my wife, Amy, and I were overdue for some adventure. Having cut my sailing teeth on sailboards and Hobie Cats, I thought this would be a nice way to take the next step up. Kentucky Bucky gave us a deal that we couldn't refuse, so we didn't. We christened her and named her in honor of Capt. Pete Lazzaro, a friend and accomplice that I cheated death with on more than one occasion. Pete was a fellow Chicagoan, sailing brother, and partner-in-adventure with me for 50-plus years from Chicago to Carbondale, Illinois, to New Orleans, to Key West and on into the Caribbean. My first trial-and-error offshore sailing was with Capt. Pete. He had just purchased a really sweet 27-foot Cape Dory sloop named *SUMMER WIND*, in honor of his idol Frank Sinatra. He, like me, was born and raised in the Lincoln Park neighborhood of Chicago. He came to me one day and said, "Hey brother, you want to go on a shakedown cruise with me on my new sailboat?"

I said, "Pete, I didn't know that you knew how to sail."

"I don't exactly, but I know you do from watching you Hobie Cat and windsurf. I know the engine and the electronics and you know how to sail and navigate."

The only appropriate thing he didn't say was "What could go wrong?"

Pete and I were both suckers for a thrill so it was a no-brainer. A-sailing we would go.

After some deliberation (and libations) we decided to wet our feet (pun intended) in the Atlantic Ocean by crossing the Gulfstream current and sailing to Bimini, which is only 60 miles east of Ft. Lauderdale and approximately 120 miles from Key West.

UNDERWAY!!! Blessed with good weather, with the exception of one pounding thunderhead, the trip was smooth with a 10-12 knot northerly wind. It was two days of idyllic sailing, warm blue water and cold Red Stripe beer.

Once we were in visual sight of Bimini, Pete raised the Bimini Big Game Club and Marina on the VHS radio. We were going to need a berth for at least one night and we also wanted to know about any unreported hazards on our approach as many sailors have sadly found that Caribbean marine charts can sometimes be dated and unreliable.

"Big Game Club, Big Game Club. This is the *SUMMER WIND*, the *SUMMER WIND*. Do you read me?"

The radio crackled a bit and then the Bahamian-accented reply came: "*SUCKING WIND, SUCKING WIND*. This is Big Game Club. We read you loud and clear."

We laughed for a week.

Actually, we're still laughing.

Pete's passed on now but remains perpetually in our hearts and spirit so, in his honor (and humor), we named our new sailboat *SUCKING WIND*.

She was moored at a little marina, just two miles from our house and on the Atlantic Ocean side (south) of the Keys, called The Geiger Key Marina and Fish Camp. It's located, as their promo proudly states, "On the Backside of Paradise." It has a bar, tiki hut restaurant, kayak rentals (ECO-TOURS), a few boat slips and you can paddle, sail or motor right in for lunch. User-friendly and remote, the kind of place you can't find unless you already know where it is.

I spent about a week just cleaning the *SUCKING WIND* up, when Amy tooled up, straddled her bike, and said, "When we going sailing, Captain?"

Always ready for a water adventure, I said, "Ready when you are mate, but we should probably wait for the highest king tide two days from now."

The king tides are unusually severe tides that occur when the sun, moon and earth are all in alignment. They happen only a few times a year but are significantly higher (and lower) by as much as 2-3 feet.

The truth is, I had sailed thousands of miles offshore doing deliveries, charters, or late-night passage (whispered: *with running lights off*), with other captains, but I had NEVER been an offshore captain myself. Now it was time to put my Big Boy Dockers on. I read and researched as much as I could about marine emergencies and preparedness. We were going to start slowly by staying just slightly offshore until we had a good feel about both the sloop, the depth and the weather, the three things that mattered immensely. The waters of the Florida Keys are notoriously shallow and even though we drew only four feet, we were happy to have a retractable/swing keel that allowed us to clear two-and-a-half feet. We sported a newly repaired mainsail and a 4-horsepower kicker (outboard motor) and were ready to get underway.

Since we lived on Big Coppitt Key on the Florida Bay (north) side of the Keys, we figured a good first endeavor would be to sail *SUCKING WIND,* from Geiger Key Marina, around the island chain to be able to dock in the canal right behind our house. Since the island-connecting bridges were too low for a sailing mast, we would have to sail all the way southwest around Key West (approximately 35 miles), or go northeast up Hawk Channel to cut west under the tallest bridge and across the Keys near

Bahia Honda (approximately 50 miles). Considering the wind and currents, we opted for the longer, but less trafficked, northeast passage.

Amy took care of the provisions. Lots of water and Gatorade to wash down our tuna, chips and peanut butter & jelly sandwiches. You can, within reason, never have too much food, water or safety gear when you go offshore (or too many peanut butter & jelly sandwiches). Even if your sailing intentions are only for a short trip. A little common sense doesn't hurt either.

It wouldn't take long before we had our first life-threatening gaffe.

We motored out of the canal at Geiger Key just past noon under a beautiful blue sky and light winds. The weather forecast was a bit "iffy" but not threatening, maybe a few scattered showers. Once we cleared the shallow coral heads we set sail. I plotted our course and we checked our heading and depth. Other than a few tall thunderheads off in the distance the conditions were ideal. I trimmed the mainsail and set the sheet in a snatch cleat and settled in. Even with a manual tiller, once we set our course, everything was basic and smooth.

And the islands began to fade in the distance behind us.

After an hour or so in the midday sun we were starting to feel the intense heat.

"Wait a second," I said, "we've got a Bimini top that we can set up to give us some shade."

I unwound the restraints on the Bimini and pulled it open over our heads.

"That's the ticket," Amy said. "I was getting cooked. That sun's pretty intense."

Eventually, even though the sea was relatively calm, the Bimini kept slipping down and exposing us to the blazing sun. The strap that held the Bimini in place had separated from years of sun and salt.

"No problem," I said. "There's a little bungee in my dive bag. Would you hand it to me please?"

I hooked the bungee onto the Bimini top and then to the nearest thing that would give it a little tension, the end of the boom. It worked just fine and we settled back in for some serious leisure time. With a light wind and outgoing tide we were on our way to deep-blue water.

As anyone who's spent hours on the water knows, a mellow sunny day can be totally relaxing and mesmerizing. Nothing but Old Sol, a few frigate birds, occasional patches of Sargassum seaweed and lots of peace and quiet. We settled onto some cushions and wallowed in our happiness and good fortune.

Amy had just started to nod into a nap and I was also getting a little sleepy-eyed, when I sensed a slight change in the air. As I turned around and peeked out from under the Bimini top, I could see an extremely dark wall of weather sneaking up fairly quickly from the west, behind us. I stood for a better look and was shocked to see how black, expansive, and thick the wall really was.

This was no isolated thunderhead but a full blown squall line.

I could feel a disconcerting uptick in the wind

as the air got noticeably cooler. *How could I have missed this on the weather report,* I thought to myself. *Oh well, I better wake Amy up and prepare to reef the main a tad, just in case it gets any windier.*

Reefing is how you reduce the area of a sail by lowering the sail and folding the excess flap at the bottom and fastening it to the boom.

Then, it hit!!!

A sudden 35-knot gust of wind slammed us like a freight train. *SUCKING WIND* heeled over violently. I lunged for the mainsheet and released it from the cleat in order to let the wind out of our mainsail. The boom swung out a foot or two to spill the wind, but then stopped suddenly, apparently impeded by something. Oh my God! The Bimini bungee was still attached to the boom! Just as Amy tried to stand up *SUCKING WIND* heeled dangerously hard to starboard and water rushed into the cockpit. Amy's feet went out from under her and she actually became airborne. When she landed in the cockpit she grabbed the cabin hatch with one hand and the lifeline with the other. Her feet were over the side, surfing on the water.

As she fought from going in the drink, I screamed, "My knife is on a hook next to the hatch. Can you reach it?" Fortunately she did, and not a moment too soon. She struggled to hand it to me while I struggled with the tiller.

I cut the bungee and the boom swung wildly to starboard. The air burst out of our sail and our mast sprung back up from a 45-degree list to upright. We looked at each other with a mixture of both shock and alarm. Simultaneously it also started pouring so hard that we could barely see with the rain pelting our eyes. Having not reefed the mainsail left us incredibly vulnerable. The wind was too much for our big main and the conditions too wild to try to reef now.

I guessed that I could probably nurse us back to the shelter of the islands if I dropped the main and used the jib. I swung windward and lowered the main. Doing so in wind that strong is high-risk for novice sailors but the alternative might have been worse. The wind and rain were so loud that we had to scream to communicate, but we eventually secured the main to the boom. The gale-force winds abated slightly to 25 knots but the seas were picking up and now lightning was starting. There were deafening booms from lightning crashing down around us like an electric hailstorm.

I was feeling more like a novice and less like a captain by the minute.

The conditions were too severe to even unroll the chart, so I just reached for the handheld GPS.

Double bummer.

The GPS had gone over the side when we heeled over. Trying to remain calm to think straight was a challenge. I knew that we had been on a broad reach, going due east for a few hours, so I tacked around to due west. At least we still had our cockpit-mounted compass. The sky was ominous and the rain was punishing. I looked down and had blood coming from one hand from when I had struggled with the knife. Fortunately, it wasn't severe, but it was just another bummer in a day that had suddenly turned on us. I flashed to one of my favorite movie lines from PREDATOR when Jesse Ventura says "I ain't got time to bleed!"

To her credit, Amy, not being a seasoned sailor, never panicked because now I needed her, and her eyes, more than ever. We were headed toward some islands that we couldn't see in the rain and, without a fathometer, we also couldn't tell the depth of the water. Between howling winds and driving rain the once crystal-clear water was now a gun-metal opaque.

Just as the sunlight was starting to fade we could barely make out some shoreline. I was guessing that it must have been the Saddlebunch Keys, about 40 miles southwest of Marathon. The rain was still coming down in sheets, the seas were boiling and the lightning was getting worse so we decided to get as close as we could to the leeward side of the islands and throw the hook to wait it out.

As we fought through waves to get near the first island, I fired up the outboard. It was pretty ancient, and not always responsive, so I was thrilled to hear her start putting. I lowered the jib and we crashed through breakers as we motored around to the lee side of the mangrove-lined barrier island.

Once in the lee, the waves laid down and the water was clearer and calmer. We could see the weed and sand bottom but could only guess at the actual depth. When we felt that we were comfortably in seven-to-ten feet of water, we threw the anchor.

We let out considerable line, "scope" in

nautical terms, in the hopes of lessening our bobbing. To make sure our hook was set, and we wouldn't drag anchor in the storm, I lowered myself over the side. We had a fluke anchor which is the most common and utile type for both small boats and sandy bottoms. We were right. It was about seven-feet deep with a sandy bottom.

The light was fading quickly now so I swam out to the anchor and dove to make sure it was set firmly.

Satisfied that we'd be secure, I swam back to the boat and had Amy lower the rope ladder for me. Anyone that's ever used a rope ladder on a boat with a fair amount of freeboard (the distance between the deck and waterline), will tell you how much they suck. I was about to find out the hard way. I grabbed the ladder and tried to step up but it just slid to the right, then I tried again and it slid to the left, then again and it went back to the right. *Son of a beach!!!*

Try as I might, I couldn't get aboard with the rope ladder. "Hey Ames! Don't we have a second rope ladder?"

"Yeah," she shouted. "I think it's in the forecastle. I'll get it." *That ought to do it. Why sell rope ladders if you can't get back in the damn boat?*

Meanwhile, the exertion and adrenaline of the day were starting to wear on me. I realized I was getting tired and weak, but I also realized I was still outside the boat and not on it...and it was getting darker. Amy brought the second rope ladder and, even in tandem, it wasn't any better. *Oh no.* I suddenly remembered reading a story about a solo-sailor that drowned because he couldn't get back on his boat. I fought back my fears because I was going to need ALL my strength and wits or this was not going to have a happy ending. I swam over to the anchor line and tried pulling myself up by that but, by now, I was way too weak and exhausted. My life didn't flash before my eyes but I did think about how embarrassingly ironic it would be to drown in seven-feet of water next to our boat.

Amy read my mind and threw me a life vest.

OH SHIT!!! While I was putting my arms though the vest something bumped my leg. A fish? A coral head? A shark?

All I could think of was the memories of my early days in Key West as a shrimper and the fact that the sharks around the Keys eat predominantly at night because that's when the food chain was more active. Sunset was long gone now and the last light was turning blue as my heart started beating faster.

I struggled desperately with the dysfunctional ladders, I couldn't get up and now I feared that drowning wasn't my biggest problem. I clung to the ropes and tried to see into the water around me. The darkness and rain made it impossible. I was talking to myself now, *Breathe. Relax. Don't be afraid of what you can't see.* Amy couldn't hide the concern on her face. I tried to focus, and then it came to me: "Amy," I yelled, "there's a hank of rope in the rear starboard hatch."

"I'm on it!"

This might've been a long shot, but it was the only shot I could think of. I tied a knot in one end of the line so that it produced a noose-like loop. Then I threw the other end to Amy.

"Take this and run it around the winch."

"Got it!"

When the line was secured I slipped my foot into the loop. "Okay, now crank the winch handle slowly while I pull up on the ladder."

OMG. Thank you Lord. I was rising slowly. *Crank, hoist, take up the slack...*and repeat. I was finally high enough to swing a leg onto the deck. Now I was completely exhausted and spent, but relieved. All I could do was lie on the deck in the pouring rain and whisper "Thanks honey, no problem."

It was dark now and the storm was gaining electrical strength. Lightning was hitting all around us again and the roar of the wind was ominous. We were both physically burnt. I suggested that maybe we should go below and try to get some sleep to wait this storm out. Then we realized that the forward cabin hatch had been open the whole time and everything below, including the bedding, was soaking wet. I had opened it earlier to let some fresh air in. Amy was not amused but, to her credit, she didn't curse me. *I certainly would have deserved it.* Not having many options, we dug out our rain ponchos and stretched out on plastic cushions in the cockpit. We pulled the hoodies closed and tried to sleep. Looking for the smallest sliver of optimism I thought: *Well at least it's not cold.*

The rain and lightning were unrelenting. At one point, lightning struck so close to us that the impact of it drove our boat sideways in the water. It was so forceful that at first I thought another boat had rammed us. It turned into a long, wet night until finally, totally drained, we both slipped into an uneasy sleep.

It was quiet and still when I first opened my eyes. It was like waking from a scary dream. The rain had not only stopped but the sky had broken up and sunrise was warming my face. I sat up and took a deep breath.

"Hey Ames. Wake up, honey. It's an absolutely gorgeous morning and the sunrise is smiling at us."

I stood up to stretch out a bit and suddenly realized *uh-oh, we're not floating anymore.* I looked over the side and, much to my horror, we were aground in only a couple feet of water. The king tide had gone out while we slept and our swing keel was partially deployed.

Then we bobbed just a little.

Because of the storm, I had no idea what the tide cycle was or even exactly where we were, so I wasn't sure if the tide had more to go out or was about to come back in. We weren't hard aground yet, so I fired up the kicker and tried to see if we could make it to deeper water, quick. Fat chance. We stirred up some sediment and then just squatted in the mud. I chuckled to myself: *This is where I thought I was going to drown last night, and now it's knee deep.*

I grinned at Amy. "Well, at least we don't have to worry about sinking or drowning."

She again was not amused, but was kind

enough to not call me an idiot. "What do you think honey?" she said. "How long do you think we're gonna be stuck here? Should I fix something to munch?"

"Hey wait a second, maybe we're in close enough to get a cell signal. We can't really get help, but we can find out about the tides and weather forecast. I'll try to call Patti Fernandez on Sugarloaf Key because she's a sailor that knows this area well."

I gave it a try.

Nothing.

Gave it another try, and "Hey, it's ringing!" After she answered, "Hi Patti. It's Will and Amy. Can you tell me what time is the next high tide on the ocean side of Saddlebunch Keys?"

"Sure," she said. "I've got the tables right here. What are y'all up to today?"

"Apparently not much," I said. "We're currently aground in the shallows out here."

When Patti finally stopped laughing, she said: "You should be good to go about two-or-three o'clock this afternoon."

I looked at my watch. It was 8 a.m. The universe was laughing at us.

Thank the Lord we had brought plenty of food and water so we didn't have to worry about that, because we were starting to get hungry and now it was starting to get hot again. We washed some freeze-dried tuna down with Gatorade, and we tried to make the most of our situation by getting out and searching for shells, on foot. Getting aboard is significantly easier when the boat is on its side in two

47

feet of water.

We climbed back aboard and rigged the now-battered Bimini top so we could have a little shade for a nap. We had a short snooze until finally Amy shouted... "Hey, we're floating again!"

Needless to say, we'd had enough fun for one day (and night) and decided to return to Geiger Key Marina rather than continue the 40-mile crossing to the bayside. I replayed every bone-headed decision and near tragedy of our last 24 hours in my head and thanked my guardian angel for working overtime. I would've had a hard time explaining to Amy's mom that I'd lost her baby girl over the side (and Amy would have never forgiven me).

The seas had lain down and a light following wind pushed us right back to our starting point. The sun was getting low as we limped into the "Backside of Paradise."

Geiger Key Marina looked like Shangri-La.

After tying up, we walked straight over to the bar. "Hi guys!" Tina asked, giving us her usual friendly smile. "Did you two have a nice sail?"

We looked at each other and laughed. "Two Anejo Tequilas, please, Tina. Better make 'em doubles."

ADDENDUM: We eventually became more conscientious sailors and had lots of fun and adventures aboard *SUCKING WIND*. Unfortunately, she met her demise in Hurricane Irma, ending up impaled by a utility pole and finally resting on our back deck. That's another story for another time.

CHAPTER #9

Man's Best Friend

Yes, I'm a dog. Born in 1946. That's what the Chinese Astrologists say anyway (okay, my wife says it too).

I imagine that's why I get along so well with other dogs, specifically the four-legged kind. I've always had at least one dog almost my entire life, except for my time in the Navy. I've had big ones (Great Danes), medium ones (Husky mixes) and little ones (Min-Pins). Their one common trait was that they were all rescues and mostly mixed-breeds.

One of my very favorites was a Husky-lab mix. He sported the beautiful Husky coat but was completely Lab black. When I went to pick him up there were other puppies trying to reach into a big water bowl for a drink, while he was actually IN the bowl having a good swim. As with so many other dogs, I loved him immediately. I named him CHAVEZ.

Chavez was one of the sweetest and gentlest animals I've ever known. He lived to be 13 and, in all my travels, he never had a leash on him in his life. It wasn't any superior training or anything on my part. We just bonded and he walked with me everywhere and would even sit by my juggling equipment while I performed. One time, while on the road out-of-state, I stopped for gas. Unbeknownst to me, Chavez jumped out of my truck to take a leak. Not realizing it, I jumped back in my truck after filling up and got back on the road. It wasn't until almost 30 miles down the road that I realized he wasn't in the back.

Holy shit!

I did a quick U-turn and sped back with my heart racing the whole way. Of course, there was Chavez sitting in the gas station right next to the pump I had used. I pulled up and he just jumped in, licked me and quietly plopped into his favorite seat, as if to say "It's okay. I knew you'd be back."

He loved kids and he loved other animals. Key West in the 80s, an island with dog friendly stores and restaurants, was the perfect place for him. The entire neighborhood loved him. Sometimes he'd just go wander around to visit people he liked while I was performing at Mallory Square. All the kids gave him the nickname BIG LOVE. If there was an ambassador for all the friendly dogs on earth it would have been BIG LOVE.

Unfortunately all dog owners, *and dogs*, aren't as loving. I had heard a rumor that some guy with a Rottweiler-mix was siccing his dog on other dogs for the thrill of watching them fight. It supposedly had happened more than once. Of course, on a small island, we would eventually encounter them. As Big Love and I were walking to Duval Street one day, I saw them approaching, the bad hombres I'd heard about, up ahead and coming at us fast. I always felt that Chavez could pick up my vibes, so I just tried to remain cool and give them a wide berth. Wrong strategy. As we passed, with Chavez walking beside me, the other dog lunged. The aggressor was probably 95 lbs., 15-20 lbs. bigger than Chavez, and grabbed him by the throat and drove him to the ground. The owner just dropped the leash. The Rottie had Big Love by the neck so, luckily, Chavez's big Husky mane probably saved his life. I grabbed the dog by the upper and lower jaw and tried to release his grip from Big Love's windpipe. It wouldn't budge. I looked at his owner and said "C'mon man, help me." Eventually, it took three of us to get the dog to release Chavez.

The owner looked at me and weakly said, "Sorry, man," and walked away dragging his dog. I knelt down next to Chavez and hugged him. He was not injured badly (bloody lip) but was obviously traumatized. I loved him up as much as I could and we went home. We were both psychically wounded.

Two days later it was all just a bad memory and things were back to normal, or so we thought. It was almost midnight and, after performing at the Sunset Celebration, I decided to join a few friends that were going to the Green Parrot for a nightcap. It was a beautiful night and the town was slow, so we walked. There was a small, locals' crowd at the Parrot and the juke box was singing the blues. As we entered past the NO SNIVELING sign, the air quickly turned from the scent of sweet night-blooming jasmine to a mix of sweaty patrons and 100 years of beer-soaked bar top. It was a steamy tropical summer night and the overworked ceiling fans were losing the battle. This was truly a working man's bar. No A/C. No blenders. No BS.

We took stools at the bar, near the door, and ordered some drafts. Chavez, as he always did, lay down next to my stool to be near my feet. No sooner than we were settling in, and who walks through the door but the Canine Wrecking Crew.

Chavez, took one look at "bad" dog and suddenly tried to get underneath my stool. Bad Dog strained at his leash to get at Chavez. I looked at the owner and said "Hey man, you can see what's happening. Will you please pull your dog away!"

He just smiled back at me and said "My dog doesn't have a problem with it. Maybe your dog does." With that he did it again. He dropped the leash and the dog sprung. It was like opening the gates of hell. The Rottie was all growling and teeth. I heard Chavez yelp as the dog grabbed him by the throat and drove him to the ground. Again.

AND I SNAPPED.

Big Love, who was the sweetest most peaceful animal I had ever known, was being savagely attacked. I was drinking ale from a beer stein when it happened, so I grabbed Bad Dog by the scruff and hit him over the head with my mug.

Nothing.

Now I'm thinking: *Holy shit, he's gonna kill Big Love.*

I hit Bad Dog again and again, until he finally

52

yelped, let go and ran away.

All of a sudden I got pulled backward. Bad Dog's owner had grabbed me by the throat and my hair. Instinctively, from years of martial arts training, I broke his grip with a spin and gave him a good roundhouse to the head.

Unfortunately for him, I still had the beer mug in my hand.

The heavy stein exploded against his head and he went down in a bloody heap. It was suddenly dead quiet in the Parrot. I think even the jukebox was stunned into silence. I looked at the bartender and said: "Would you please call him an ambulance."

Looking back, there was a brief moment of levity when the guy who had been sitting next to me stood up and said "CHECK PLEASE!"

I went outside and sat on the curb to wait for the ambulance and the inevitable police. After the paramedics had treated and had taken Bad Dog Owner away and the police interviewed and subsequently arrested me, I was being handcuffed when I suddenly realized that Chavez was gone. I looked anxiously around but he was nowhere to be seen.

The police were professional and courteous but explained to me that since a *weapon* was used, they were going to have to charge me with aggravated battery. They took me to lockup and my bond was set at $50,000. All I could think of all night was Chavez. In the morning, I was informed that the detectives had questioned all the witnesses who had unanimously agreed that I was just reacting in self-defense and they dropped the charges and released me. But what about Chavez? My heart was racing and breaking. He was part of my family. He was the Big Love, and he was gone. First thing I needed to do was check the animal shelter.

After that I would put up some posters and start scouring the island. I made my way back to my truck to start the search and, as I fumbled in my pocket for the keys, I heard a familiar sound from under the truck.

You guessed it. Big Love crawled out and gave me his paw and a big lick as if to say "It's okay. I knew you'd be back."

Going forward, the good news was that Bad Dog got banned from the Parrot.

Unfortunately, ALL dogs were then banned from the Parrot. I even got a one month suspension. Chavez still accompanied me there after our sentence though, but was happy to sit outside the open door and next to the dog-friendly water bowl.

And, in the Key West spirit, both of us are still getting thank-you drinks from many of the other local dog lovers. My only regret is for that poor dog that was trained to fulfill his sadistic owner's bad intentions.

Given the chance, Big Love could've, and would've, been his buddy.

CHAPTER #10

Aaargh!!!

When you grow up in the Midwest, a thousand miles from any seacoast, the ocean can be incredibly intimidating.

I remember the first time being on a boat whose depth finder was signaling 2,000 feet. I couldn't stop thinking that there was only a thin layer of fiberglass between me and the abyss. It took me awhile to realize that there's no difference between 7 feet and 7,000 feet. If it's over your head, it's over your head. I also wasn't a strong swimmer but, when you're 100 miles offshore, that's not much of an issue either.

It took me literally thousands of hours to make my peace with the ocean but, when I finally did, it opened up a whole new universe to me.

It didn't come easily or naturally though, especially at a time when the movie *JAWS* was a smash hit and I still didn't trust anything I couldn't see even in knee-deep water. More and more I noticed that my local swimming and diving buds, those who grew up in the Keys swimming before they could walk, were so totally relaxed in the water. That was my epiphany. Relaxation.

Snorkeling was the first baby step, or dive. Snorkeling's great for people who are just getting to know the ocean. You don't have to worry about drowning because you're already floating face down, and you're breathing fine. And you don't have to worry about what mystery could possibly be under the surface because you're actually looking at it. It's that moment of Zen when you finally relax and suddenly realize…you've just passed through to another universe.

I mean seriously.

Your breathing slows down and your body starts to move differently, slower, more in tune with your breath and the currents. The saltwater wants to lift and float you, and when you finally surrender to that buoyancy, you've successfully slipped the bounds of gravity. Eureka! It's really close to flying, but through different matter.

So now you've relaxed and here comes your next delightful discovery. Oh My GOD! There are fish of every color and size, from loners to schools of thousands. And they're synchronized swimming around vividly colored coral heads that are found everywhere in the Florida Keys' shallow inshore waters. Corals of every shape, size and hue stretch as far as the eye can see. Truly, this is another universe and now it was becoming friendly instead of fearful. As usual, I wanted more.

The next step was learning how to enjoy

myself on the surface, as well. It seemed to me that the happiest people on the beach were the windsurfers. It's a great concept. Learn to sail by actually holding the sail in your hands. Simple, right? Well, except for having to stand on a floating board that's bobbing on the waves, and having to balance yourself against that sail while the wind keeps shifting and gusting. Haha, after six months of pulled muscles, bruises from falling and missing the ocean (landing on your board), broken toes and an extreme lesson in humility; I was finally a competent windsurfer.

That humility lesson was key. The day that I realized I was dancing with the wind, but that the wind was leading and not me, I relaxed once again and the joy of sailing was orgasmic.

As with any passion, the weeks turned into months and then into years. I think I was pretty much a windsurfing beach bum for those next four-to-five years. I performed just enough at the Sunset Celebration to pay for eating and drinking that night, with just enough money left for a morning cafe con leche before sailing all day again. Was this the same ocean that used to scare the doo out of me? Slowly and unintentionally I was falling in love with her.

For those of us who were hooked on board-sailing it floated somewhere between a passion and an obsession. We sailed in the day and we sometimes sailed at night. We were ready to go whenever the wind was ready. We sailed on lazy breezes and we sailed in crazy storms, and you had to have special equipment for different conditions. Smaller storm sails for handling big wind coupled with smaller boards for less drag made breath-taking speeds possible.

One day, my windsurfing sister (Patti Fernandez), who was a sailor, sail-maker and adventurer, made me a unique storm-sail for my birthday that was all black. She asked our artist friend, Tony Gregory, to draw up a big white skull-and-crossbones which she inlaid into the center of the flag, making it a perfect pirate-flag sail. It was perfect for sailing in the waters where actual pirates once thrived. My fantasies and realities were starting to blend. Keep in mind this was the middle 80s.

Flash forward 20 years. Time does fly when you're living your dreams. Eventually I graduated to Hobie Cats and mono-hulled sailboats and was lucky enough to sail throughout the Caribbean on several different sized sailboats as crew.

Right after one of those sailing trips, I met Amy, the amazing partner I always wanted and definitely needed. We just celebrated our 20th wedding anniversary so I guess I can say we're starting to get the hang of it. But in those early years we were trying, like so many other couples, to decide where and how we wanted to live. Should we try to buy a house in Key West? Or should we look elsewhere? Haha, FAT chance. We were both hopelessly in love with Key West, it being both of ours adopted home, and that was that. We'd put our roots down in Cayo Hueso, the only community either of us ever felt like calling home.

We started to search the housing market in

the lower Keys. We looked at everything from Conch houses to condos to floating houseboats. Even in the early 2000s real estate was starting to rise quickly. We figured we had a decent down payment (10 percent) in the neighborhood of our price range. Now all we had to do was find financing.

Welcome back to reality. I had a good steady income, but not enough of a paper trail. The banks would each explain to me that the problem wasn't that I had bad credit. It was that I didn't have ANY credit. I had been living in a cash and carry world for so long that I had insufficient documentation of my income. So slowly I began the credit-dance by taking-and-then-paying secured loans. It's a process so I started it.

Meanwhile, I happened to mention my plight to my close friend and highly respected real estate attorney, Richard Klitenick. While we were working out at the Tae Kwon Do dojang in Key West, he said to me: "I have a good friend in Miami who's a private mortgage broker. You should give him a ring. Maybe he can help you."

I hesitated at first because this was all new to me and I was sort of tired of getting shown the door by mortgage bankers. But sometimes the fun is in the hunt so, in the spirit of nothing-ventured nothing-gained, Amy and I thought *Why not?*

I called the gentleman, who I'll call Bruce, and began to pitch my predicament. I explained that I had been performing steadily for close to 25 years in Key West and had lived there that entire time. I considered my income reasonable, modest and steady yet I didn't have much verification of that. I did however have $25,000 for a down payment on a house in the $250,000-$275,000 range. Then I waited for the inevitable "Well. I'm sorry, I can't help you."

There was silence for a moment, and then a small chuckle. "Will," Bruce said, "I know who you are and what you do for a living. I used to live in Key West, and occasionally watched you on the high wire."

"Now," he continued, "I'm going to tell you a story I've wanted to tell you for many years.

"I was a newbie windsurfer in the 80s," he explained. "I was just getting enough confidence to get a couple miles offshore on a beautiful sun-filled day. The wind wasn't screaming, but it was blowing steadily and I was enjoying a broad reach that was taking me due south. Suddenly, at about three-to-four miles offshore, a sharp gust blew and my outhaul, the little rope that ties the clew of your sail to your booms, just snapped."

(*Without that outhaul there was no way to keep wind in the sail.*)

"I was now sitting on my board with no wind power and being pulled slowly out to sea by an outgoing tide. I'd been drifting for several hours but there were no boats in the immediate area and I was beginning to get nervous. Key West was getting smaller. As I passed the reef, at seven miles, the color change from aqua to deep blue was ominous. Was I entering the 5 mph Gulfstream current? As I considered my very few options, I saw something far off that looked vaguely like another windsurfer. As it got closer my feelings of relief turned to consternation. It was another windsurfer but he was flying a pirate sail. Holy crap. Not only was I being pulled out to sea but now I was possibly about to be boarded and robbed by some rogue sailor."

He paused, then:

"You do remember now that sailor was you, don't you Will? You sailed in a big circle around me and then came alongside and said 'Are you Okay?'"

"I explained what had happened to my rig. Then you smiled, sailed up, dropped your mast and sat down on your board. First things first, you said, and pulled a water container out of your harness and passed it to me. Without missing a beat you then pulled a small piece of rope out of your life vest pocket which we used to re-attach my clew. Next, to my delight, you pulled out a waterproof container and said 'You could probably use this too.' Right there and then we smoked some ritual herbs to celebrate a successful rescue at sea. The sail back to Key West was both therapeutic and bonding."

Then he revealed something that I'll never forget. "I've often thought about how badly that day could have turned out if you hadn't shown up when you did and, for that reason...I'm going to lend you a quarter of a million dollars for your house."

Thank you Bruce, for the Key West pirate cred and for the most incredible tip I ever received. Thank you Rich Klitenick for the valuable advice. Thank you Mother Ocean for your generous bounty. Thank you Key West for being a catalyst for magic.

And thank you Patti F. for teaching me to keep a spare piece of rope with me at all times.

CHAPTER #11

Halloween. Trick or Treat?

In my 43 years of performing on Mallory Square in Key West, I've met hundreds of zany, creative and talented folks doing unbelievable feats of derring-do, prestidigitation and just plain nuttiness. This next experience has a bit of everything.

As with any profession, you really never get to know people that you see every day. But there are those individuals to whom you simply gravitate. You become friends instantly and comfortably.

It was like that when I met Michael Patrick. Tall, long-haired and muscular, he had a friendly face, honest eyes and a loving dog. That dog part's always been important to me for the obvious reasons. Dog lovers, for the most part, respect other animals and I've always trusted my own dogs' instincts when certain people make their tail wag. Michael is one of those people.

Michael was an escape artist. He would allow his audience to secure him in a straightjacket and then wrap him in chains. The chains were then locked in several spots and tested by his volunteers to make sure he was rolled as tight as a cornhusk-wrapped tamale. After that, his ankles were bound with rope. Then came the REAL challenge. Up until this point, the audience had been left wondering what the 15-foot steel tripod behind Michael was for. As instructed, the volunteers then hooked Mike up by his ankles to a cable winch connected to the top of the tripod. Once secured, another audience participant would slowly turn the ratchet handle until Michael began to lift off the ground and eventually hang inverted, with his head 7-8 feet above the concrete. His escape was always gut-wrenching, crowd-pleasing and successful. Night after night, his performance beat the odds and his audience loved it because they both identified with him and just as importantly, he also made them laugh. Of course, as a true born Florida boy, he also completed the entire feat in his flip-flops. He was irresistible.

One night, as we sat at the water's edge waiting for our time to perform, Michael reminded me that it was Halloween and that his idol, Harry Houdini, had died on Halloween. He also made a fleeting reference to wanting to honor him some day in a performance. I filed the bucket-list thought in the "whatever" folder.

Then, as the sun sank lower, it was SHOWTIME. By the luck of the draw, I went first that night. The energy was good, the crowd was enthusiastic and I had a safe and enjoyable show juggling fire on the tight-wire. I thanked my crowd and reminded them to enjoy the other shows that were coming up next, particularly Michael who was set up next to me.

A few minutes went by as I picked up my equipment and settled back into my fold-out camp chair to catch my breath. Then I heard it...a loud SPLASH!

I looked over to the pitch next to me, where Michael, should be doing his show, and noticed that most of his crowd had walked over to the pier's edge and were looking down into the water. I thought to myself: *Oh great, some drunk probably fell in and interrupted Michael's show and distracted his crowd.*

I walked over to where they were all staring down into the water: "Did someone fall or jump in?"

A girl next to me said: "It was the escape guy. He's doing an underwater escape."

A chill went through me because 1) I knew Michael had never done an underwater escape, and 2) I also knew the channel was 40 feet deep there with wicked currents. In a panic I asked her if he had his straightjacket and chains on and she cried "YES!"

As I ripped off my shirt and shoes, I yelled "He doesn't do underwater escapes. Someone call 911!" and I then yelled for the neighboring performer over to spread the word. That next performer was a Hungarian mime name Jozsef Burai. He dove in with me. The tide was RIPPING. It must have been 4-5 knots as it funneled through the channel. The surging tide was making the water so cloudy that you literally couldn't see your hand in front of your face. Every time I thought I might be looking at what might be Michael in the murkiness, I'd reach out and grab a barnacle-encrusted piling under the pier. Bummer! When I came up for air, I noticed Jozsef was getting washed down the pier by the current and yelled to him to grab a ladder that he was drifting past. He just managed to get a hand on the ladder before he too would have been in need of a rescue. The conditions were worsening.

We did our best. We dove until it felt like my lungs would bleed. Then I felt a big splash next to me and realized someone with scuba tanks had jumped in the water. Thank God, it was the Police and Fire Department dive team. After them came the Florida Marine Patrol divers and eventually the Coast Guard. The Coast Guard actually sent a helicopter down from Miami. I was impressed with all the divers' coordination and professionalism. They immediately set up a grid and used ropes and spotlights as more surface craft joined in the search.

Jozsef and I climbed back onto the pier and sat stunned. Overcome by heat and exhaustion, we both started vomiting salt water. The nightmare of our reality was sinking in.

Michael was one of the most liked people on Mallory Square. People were huddled together and crying while they tried to comfort each other. Was it a trick gone awry? Or was it possibly a suicide? The poor people from his crowd, who were the volunteers that tied him up in his straightjacket, were overwrought. We sat there until midnight. No Michael. The divers were starting to come out of the water now and announced that they would resume the search at daybreak. The bleak reality that this was no longer considered a rescue, but a recovery effort, was crushing.

Something was bothering me though. As I looked around, several things didn't quite add up. The first was that his faithful dog, Lena, was nowhere to be seen. He never went ANYWHERE without Lena. If she wasn't allowed somewhere, Michael wouldn't go there. Secondly, his Busker's hat, which is passed for tips, was nowhere to be seen. No veteran Busker would do a show without his hat on hand. Thirdly, no cell phone in his remaining pile of equipment on the pier. Did someone make off with all that stuff in the excitement and confusion? But Lena wouldn't go with a stranger. Then, when I was finally too tired to make sense of it all, I cut through the parking lot to leave and realized that his car was missing also. I knew I was exhausted and overly emotional, but I couldn't get over the nagging feeling that there were too many unanswered questions.

I went home, changed clothes and poured a huge snifter of Grand Marnier. As I sat down at my kitchen table to gather my thoughts...my phone rang. I looked down at the caller ID...and it was Michael.

"How did you like my tribute to Houdini?" he said triumphantly.

"HOLY SHIT MICHAEL!" I yelled into the phone. "First things first, I'm thrilled and relieved that you're alive." The next things I explained to him were important too though. "I don't need to know the details of your trick, but you need to know that all of your friends are crying and grieving because they think you're dead. You're supposed to appear at the end of that trick.

"But even more importantly, there are divers that are going back down looking for you at first light. Those guys are risking their necks in dangerous currents for you. You MUST go and turn yourself in as soon as we hang up."

There was silence on the phone for a second, then he acquiesced "I promise to turn myself in first thing in the morning if you'll promise not to tell anyone I called." I told him okay, as long as he did it before the divers went back down.

I threw the Grand Marnier down, and then had another one. It was going to be hard to get any sleep. With all the adrenalin I had pumped, it was impossible.

At sunrise, as usual, I walked my dogs down to my local *cafecito* for some cafe con leche, where someone startled me with: "I read about you diving for your friend last night, I'm sorry you didn't find him."

It was then that I realized the whole thing was splashed across the front page of the *Key West Citizen*!

My heart raced. *HOLY GUACAMOLE! I'm the only one that knows he's alive!*

I could imagine what was going to happen next. I ran home and told Amy to pack me a sandwich while I grabbed an overnight bag and jumped into my truck. I was on the highway in minutes and didn't stop until I reached Orlando, frantically calling Michael all the way. Amy called me with updates. "Jeezus," she said, "you just got out of here and the phone started ringing non-stop. The *Miami Herald*, the *New York Times*, UPI, AP, etc. I told them you were on the road and couldn't be reached."

Gotta love that girl.

Eventually, of course, Michael was arrested and charged with several misdemeanors for which he was fined and sentenced to 60 days in the Monroe County hoosegow.

Days later, when I visited Michael in jail, I told him he should have received an award for the most amazing stunt ever performed at Mallory Square, but also deserved the sentence for not vetting the ending a little better. He's still waiting for the award.

Well...he *did* forewarn me that he had wanted to do something that people would never forget.

Mission accomplished, Michael.

We still love and miss you here in Key West.

Safe travels, wherever you are.

CHAPTER #12

Rock Festival

I find it interesting that my work itinerary correlates directly to my age. As I grow older, I travel less and less for work, opting to have as much time at home for my favorite hobbies of gardening and Everglades kayaking. My love for adventure kayaking in the 'Glades could fill three books, but right now, this particular tale is about gardening/landscaping in the Florida Keys, and how exciting that can actually become.

Growing things in the tropics is a pure joy. When I lived in the Midwest, I could kill a plant in world-record time, but things are much different the closer you get to the Equator. The biodiversity changes immensely. Instead of spending lots of focus and energy (like up north) merely keeping plants alive, I spend more time trimming and cutting back things that are growing too fast. The heat and humidity coupled with *beaucoup* sunshine and a twelve-month frost-free growing season are the driving factors. But actually, international trade and the maritime industry also had lots to do with the variety of tropical agriculture in both Florida and Central America.

Orange juice, for example, has become synonymous with Florida over the past 75 years. I had always assumed that it was a native plant, endemic to the Florida peninsula, but I was wrong. Oranges never existed in Florida until the mid-1500s when they were imported from Spain, purportedly by Ponce de Leon. It took almost 400 years for them to develop into a cash crop and an identifiable brand for the Sunshine State. I love orange juice. Thank you *Señor* de Leon.

Bananas were another stumper for me. Bananas, which I also love, have become so representative of Central America that we've even coined the term "Banana Republic" in reference to some of their trade and politics. But, again, bananas were also introduced to Central America and the Caribbean by international traders from Southeast Asia. Bananas were thought to have originated in India. It wasn't until the late 1800s that their mass cultivation here took root (no pun intended).

So it should come as no surprise that I have both oranges (Valencia & navel) and five varieties of bananas growing in our yard. We also have papayas, guava, Key limes, mangoes and Barbados cherries. They all LOVE the sun. We also have various vegetables and herbs but they, of course, like a little more shade. Having two distinct growing seasons, winter and summer, makes things twice as nice. But, as much as I love eating the fruits of our labor, I think the part of gardening I enjoy the most is the flowers. Colorful, fragrant and exotic, the flowers are the diamonds in the garden.

Twelve months a year of flowers blooming was one of the things that overwhelmed me when I first came to the Keys in February 1976. The air was always sweet with gardenias in the day and jasmine at night. A month later, the multi-colored frangipani and burning red royal Poincianas bloomed and the entire island was blanketed in colors both soothing and vivid. I felt as if I were wearing tinted glasses (and the orchids hadn't even started yet).

It's not hard to see how I succumbed to gardening fever. Fortunately for me, my wife Amy has a green thumb no matter where she lives so we became a gardening team. As we grew we learned, and as we learned we grew. Pretty soon we were running out of space. It was that reality that taught us the relationship between gardening and landscaping.

Having studied art and design at Southern Illinois University, you could say I bloomed quickly (OK, pun was intended that time). In order for our tropical garden to be accessible, enjoyable and therapeutic, it needed some biotic feng shui. It begged for a waterfall and some imaginative walkways.

That's where this particular story took a strange twist.

Influenced by one of my favorite Key West artists/sculptors, Carolyn Gorton Fuller, I envisioned an eclectic walkway made from discarded materials. Carolyn was the artist that created the famous "Bottle Wall" bordering her property next to the Key West Cemetery. The wall was constructed with an assortment of different sized and colored glass bottles (and other glass objects) and held together with dribbled cement. It was a visually stimulating marriage of beauty, form and function. Finding the materials for our pathway became an adventure.

Anywhere else, flat river stones would have been suitable but the Keys' base is limestone and there are no stones or rocks. As Ms. Carolyn would say: *It was time for some serious "dumpster diving."*

Needing flat tile-like shapes of any and all materials, we got our boots and gloves on, and we scoured every empty lot, deserted shoreline and construction site/dump that we could find. Little by little and week by week, a mosaic walkway started to form through our private Eden until we were almost through. With only ten feet left to finish, we embarked on one last search for art-construction material treasure. From Key West to Big Coppitt Key (mile-marker 10) we had already rummaged in every nook imaginable. Now we were just roaming and exploring.

Stock Island, Key West's closest neighbor sometimes referred to as "rock island," had a reputation as a 24-hour crack cocaine dispensary.

As Amy and I drove the back streets of the island, I noticed a locked and gaited road that led back through the mangroves. I'd seen it before but happened to notice that for the first time the gate was now open. "Aha, this could be our mother lode."

I drove right in and began to idle down the overgrown dirt lane, scanning the brush for trash or treasure.

It was then that I saw two vans, side by side, stopped about 100 yards down the road ahead of us. My heart raced suddenly as I considered the possibility that we had just unwittingly stumbled onto a clandestine drug transaction. I slowed to a stop. The path was too narrow for a U-turn. Before I could put my old Tacoma in reverse, one of the vans started up and sped toward us. *Oh shit!*

The van raced right up next to us and the tinted driver's window powered down. A dark-clothed man in aviator shades, who was not smiling, demanded: "What the hell are you doing back here?"

Nervous, and wanting to be accommodating, I blurted out "We're just looking for some rocks!"

Before I could say "Let me re-phrase that," he jumped out with handcuffs at the ready, and identified himself as a Monroe County Narcotics operative. *Double Oh Shit!* He was both intent AND excited, like a fisherman who'd just hooked a big one (or was maybe having *MIAMI VICE* fantasies).

Slowly, I produced my local Driver's License and introduced myself and my wife. I explained the nature of our project, showed him some of the rock-like junk in my truck bed that we had already found and then showed him photos of our almost completed walkway. He was not amused, but returned my license, and scowled for us to leave immediately.

It was a half mile before I quit sweating and we started laughing. We drove home and sat chuckling in front of the smiling Buddha in our private Zen-garden.

Who knew landscaping could be so exciting?

CHAPTER #13

A Good Paddling Never Hurt Anyone

When Amy and I first started hanging out together in the mid 90s, I was still an avid windsurfer. The problem was that board surfing is an individual's sport. One board equals one person. In order to solve that problem, and enjoy playing together, we starting sailing Hobie catamarans. Although it propelled Amy off the beach and kept us together, it was still me doing the sailing and her sunbathing. We loved our time on the water together but she needed to be more involved.

Welcome to the Kayak Era.

Kayaks are indeed a great way to experience the water world.

1) They're quiet and animal friendly. Without the roar of an engine, one can interrelate with all sorts of fish, marine mammals and birds without disrupting their peaceful habitats.

2) They're environmentally friendly with NO emissions, and a minimal carbon footprint.

3) They're portable, requiring no dockage.

4) They're versatile. Depending on your intentions and usage (open water, river rapids, etc.), kayaks can be made from a number of different materials from wood or fiberglass to the practically indestructible plastic, Polyethylene (think old Tupperware). There are even inflatable ones.

5) Prices, weights and shapes can all vary to suit your individual needs. They're available as singles or tandems.

6) They're reasonably priced from several hundred to several thousand dollars. Throw in some paddles and life-vests and you're good to go. The fresh air and water are free.

7) It's healthy! Whether you just want to relax or go for a challenging workout, you can pick your location, weather conditions and distance according to your desires that day.

8) No registration fees or licensing (in Florida anyway).

We picked out a couple of single Old Town Polyethylene kayaks that were tailored to our individual heights, leg lengths and weights. We chose boats with foot-controlled rudders to help us navigate ocean tides and river currents. We've used them constantly for 20 years and they're still ready to go at a moment's notice.

The clear turquoise waters around Key West are teeming with colorful fish, beautiful corals, sponges and all shapes of sea shells…and that's just for openers. In all my years of kayaking in south Florida, I almost always see something that's new, interesting and remarkable every time we go out.

Add to that the endless adventure of the neighboring Everglades and you have a lifetime of exploration possibilities.

We started out in the shallow (two-to-five feet) inshore waters of the Florida Keys. If you're inexperienced or accidentally capsize, you're not in any danger of drowning. Just stand up. There are very few things that pose any danger there.

A great place to get your chops down is a little used area of shallows and mangroves tucked back as a buffer behind the Key West airport. We often refer to it as "lunchtime Costa Rica." This series of waterways is part of a now-abandoned, salt-pond system by which, through evaporation, Key West once harvested its salt. Entry is through narrow mangrove canals that are canopied, creating an enchanting tunnel entrance into an idyllic, tropical habitat. The shallow water inhibits propellers which helps maintain the peaceful experience, interrupted only occasionally by minimal aircraft traffic from the airport.

The remote mangrove passageways serve as nurseries for both fish and birds. It's a safe place for juveniles to grow and adapt before they go out into the full ocean and come face to face with all its toothy predators. The seabed in the pond is covered with beautiful jellyfish and anemones, some which closely resemble the flower Queen Anne's lace. It's a veritable wonderland of biodiversity that most Key Westers have never even seen but, if you have a kayak, you can access it on your lunch hour (okay, two hours).

If you live in or travel to the Florida Keys and enjoy kayaking, you will NEVER run out of new places to discover. There are literally hundreds of island destinations, many of them remote, which are available to explore. After ten-plus years of paddling, snorkeling and camping throughout the island chain, we considered it our therapy and always love to share it with our friends and guests.

Then one day, while heading north for an autumn North Carolina vacation, Amy and I were driving across the southern Everglades on the Tamiami Trail. As we were crossing the Miccosukee Indian Village it started pouring rain like it does in the jungle. It was a rain that would open a new world for us. It was raining so hard that we thought stopping for lunch in Everglades City would be a good idea to chill out and let the thunderheads pass.

Everglades City is a tiny town (population 400 or so) that is located in Everglades National Park and the Big Cypress Swamp. I had once read of a century-old historic lodge there named the Everglades Rod and Gun Club which was a place dignitaries, luminaries and bigwigs could find relaxation, recreation and privacy away from the bright lights of media and the rat race. Sounded good to us so we searched it out. A once-grand hotel in stature, it sat tucked away into the backside of town and right on a waterway. The main hotel was closed for repairs but cabins were still available...and they had a restaurant. Sign us up!

While we lunched there, we struck up a conversation with a local kayak guide. She gave us some tips, maps and some insider local preferences. *Awesome,* we thought. *Perhaps we should just hang here for a few days and check it out.*

It was one of our all-time best decisions.

The rain slowed to a drizzle, which was a big plus because it kept all the bugs grounded. We were pulling a small trailer with our own kayaks and equipment so we decided to launch and take a quick peek at the surrounding area. What we found was the stuff of dreams.

The Big Cypress Swamp is the type of swamp I always pictured as a kid. The huge cypress trees form a canopy that transforms even the brightest sunny day into a mysterious, dark and shady wonderland of wild orchids, Spanish moss, exotic birds and LOTS of alligators. It took us about 30 minutes to decide to stay a few days and see more.

The guide from the Rod and Gun Club had said "If you want a good long paddle to get a good feel for the Big Cypress Swamp, try the Turner River. It runs south from Tamiami Trail (Route 41) and winds through cypress swamps, mangrove tunnels and brackish bays for about eight or nine miles. It'll take you six-to-seven hours until it ends at Chokoloskee, an old Indian shell island, but it'll be worth it."

There was even someone on Chokoloskee who you could call to trailer yourselves and your equipment back to your vehicle at the launch site. That was good news because Chokoloskee (I love that name) is as far as any road goes back into the Big Cypress Swamp. We were stoked. Filled with anticipation, we both had a hard time sleeping that night.

The next morning we were up at first light and started the day with a hearty breakfast from the Island Cafe, a great biscuits-and-gravy spot that was teeming with fishermen and guides who were munching down while planning their day's strategy. The weather was perfect, not too hot, and there was a nice breeze to keep the bugs at a minimum. As you may have guessed, the conditions for bugs and weather can either enhance your trip or make it miserable. You need to prepare for both.

We stopped at the Everglades Park Ranger Station and dropped off our required Float Plan. There's no fee but the idea is similar to a flight plan for aircraft. It's definitely a wilderness area so, if you don't come out after an allotted time, they want to know approximately where to look for you.

We gathered our gear with one last inventory check: Food, water, insect repellent, rain gear, first-aid kit (with EPI-pens), knives, camera, rope and smart phones in waterproof Pelican boxes. Interestingly enough, and to our grateful surprise, we were able to get a cell signal for almost the whole excursion. Our safety fears were somewhat allayed (always expect the unexpected) and we excitedly pushed off.

My first memorable impression was the serenity. Once we were a mere 15 minutes from the launch site, we never heard or saw another Human Being until we reached Chokoloskee seven hours later. Except for the birds, there was total peace and quiet. There was, however, NO shortage of wildlife: Gators, birds of all types and sizes, raccoons, turtles, deer, crabs, etc. Even though we knew from news reports that invasive species of large snakes, mostly pythons, were also propagating in the Everglades, we didn't see any in person. We did, however, see the long, crusty snakeskins they had shed, which kept us laser vigilant. Thankfully, the bugs were keeping a low profile. The air was heavy and sweet. The smell was like a tropical greenhouse and most all the trees had flowering bromeliads attached to them. It was a scene that hadn't changed for untold millennium.

Alligators have been on earth for 200-million years. They've actually outlived dinosaurs by 65-million years. It's hard to look at them and not imagine them as present-day dinosaurs. We saw gators of all sizes, some as big as ten-to-twelve feet, and they were everywhere. On the banks, in the reeds, and in the water all around us. They weren't threatening though. I imagined them looking at us, the same way we in the Keys look at sun-burned tourists from up north, and rolling our eyes. The closer we passed to them the more comfortable I started feeling. A small one, between three-to-four feet, actually slid down the bank and swam over to Amy's boat. He pulled right up to her and started swimming alongside her, like a little pet dog. *These gators are getting a bad rap,* I thought to myself. The more of them I saw, the more hospitable they seemed.

Then it happened.

Amy was crossing some fairly shallow flats

with an orangish muddy bottom. BOOM! BOOM! Amy's kayak made two loud thumps as if she'd hit something. She had. While her boat rocked side-to-side precariously, a startled gator, that had been lying on the mud bottom, came flying out frantically from under her. I think he was even more startled than she was. He scrambled up onto the bank, presumably cursing us tourists in gator-talk. Amy finally exhaled. I asked her if she was alright and she just laughed and said, "I'm okay but I think I may have to change my pants."

"Make that two of us," I laughed. "That was more adrenaline than a run with the bulls. That was EPIC!"

The sun was straight overhead now and we both needed something to calm our nerves so we decided to stop for lunch and a breather. We pulled our boats up on a shady hammock island and took a long-overdue stretch. As our adrenaline began to subside, we broke out some Gatorade and trail mix. We both chuckled about the new adventure story we'd have for our friends. We still had a fair ways to go though so, after some self-medication, we pushed back in and continued our journey.

The water was getting deeper now as we neared Florida Bay and Chokoloskee, and the wildlife was changing. The gators were bigger but so were the birds. We saw blazing pink roseate spoonbills, often mistaken for flamingos, as well as deer-sized wood storks and great blue herons. The mid-day stillness was interrupted only by the peeps of a solitary osprey diving for his own lunch. I hoped the pictures I was taking would do them justice.

As I passed some gorgeous water lilies in full bloom, I grabbed for my camera. As I turned and leaned for a better angle, suddenly…SPLASH!

OH NO!

My kayak capsized!

Instantly, all those benevolent and warm feelings I was having about gators vanished from my head only to be replaced with a quiet anticipatory dread, again similar to the movie *JAWS*.

I tried not to move too fast, like an animal in distress would, so as not to attract too much attention. Amy was far enough in front of me that she wasn't even aware of what had happened. My kayak righted itself but was now full of water so I couldn't get back in. The tea-colored water was clear and dark but deep. It was eerily quiet. I looked around and tried to remember where the last gator I had seen was swimming. Frighteningly enough, he was the biggest one I had spied all day. Every time my toes touched something I'd recoil like a long rifle. Then I heard Amy calling to me. She never liked it when she couldn't see me, and now only my head was out of the water. I didn't want to yell or stress her (or the gators) out, but neither did I want to be gator bait. Amy paddled up, but what could she do? If she tried to help me up it would only capsize her too. Ironically, I suddenly thought of one of the guides jokingly say, "If you and your friend fall in the water next to a gator…you don't have be faster than the gator. You only have to be faster than

84

your friend."

This was a lot funnier back at the cafe.

Anyway, I swam slowly and pulled myself up onto the muddy shore and secured my kayak on some cypress knees, the cone-shaped buttress roots at the base of the bald cypress trees. What a mess, but at least it wasn't cold. When I finally caught my breath, Amy and I had a good laugh. We lost my camera, but not our sense of humor. As we used to say in sports, *no harm...no foul.*

We bailed my boat out and got back on our way, a lot muddier but with all my appendages. Are we having fun yet? Are the alligators laughing at us?

Well, we came for an adventure and we were definitely getting our money's worth. The last stretch was across an open bay to Chokoloskee in the distance. We were in our seventh hour and by that time both of our shoulders were starting to burn. When we finally reached shore we were so tired we just dragged our boats out and lay in the sea grass staring up. As if we needed any more magical signs, there were not one, but two huge owls sitting on a tree branch right over our heads.

"Look Ames," I said. "It's the welcome wagon."

Amy just smiled and gave me a kiss. Exhausted, wet, muddy but extremely happy, we both knew that this was just the beginning of our love affair with the Everglades and the Big Cypress Swamp.

To paraphrase Douglas MacArthur..."We shall return."

CHAPTER #14

GOD is DOG

Okay, let's just start right out by saying that there are relatively few things in this world cuter, cuddlier and sweeter smelling than a puppy.

I admit it, I'm a sap when it comes to four-legged fur babies with wagging tails. Sometimes when I read about someone "found living with 76 dogs" I think to myself "Yep, I get it."

I've been privileged to host 16 different (and I mean different) dogs in my life. Everything from Great Danes to Miniature Pinschers, from newborns to seniors…and all of them rescues. Some were from shelters, some from troubled or abandoned homes, one from a yard sale and all of them needing me, apparently, as much as I needed them.

I'm not going to go in depth on all of them here, even though each one has its own special story. I will, however, share some of my favorite memories with you. I will also pay homage to them all by listing their names here with a heartfelt thank you and tail wag, for all the love and companionship we shared through the years.

1) "Tippy" — Beagle/Terrier mix
2) "Rudy" — Beagle/Basset mix
3) "Colonel Frank Lee Macuba" — Boston Harlequin Dane
4+5) "Babe" & "Buddy Miles" — Brindle Great Danes
6) "Big Mama Thornton" — black Great Dane
7) "Kenosha" — Malamute/Huskie mix
8) "Chavez" (the Big Love) — Huskie/Lab mix
9) "Buchi" — black & tan Min-Pin
10) "Frodo Baggins" — red Min-Pin
11) "Belle" — Malinois (Belgian Shepherd)
12) "Sam" — black & tan Min-Pin
13) "Squiggy" — Maltese mix
14) "Cisco Kid" — Miniature Rat Terrier
15) "Henny Penny" — Terrier mix
16) "Lilly" — Little Black Cutie Pie

My all-time favorite, of course, was Chavez, the Big Love. I've already covered a Chavez story in this book, but he also figures in some of the other stories as we go on.

I'll start out with one of the biggest dogs I've ever known: COLONEL FRANK LEE MACUBA. Boston Harlequin is a color scheme much like a Holstein cow, big blotches of black and white. Frank was nearly as big as a cow too. He was huge, 155 lbs. of muscle and, crazily enough, he was a rescue. Thank God he was mellow. He got the name Frank because of a perfect black "F" on the white side of his neck. He got the title "Colonel" because of his undying love of fried chicken.

Someone from Florida, who was going away on a long federal vacation, gave him to me while I was seasonally living in a basement apartment in Rogers Park, a Chicago lakefront neighborhood.

Normally a goliath dog and a basement apartment are not a good mix, but Frank had a good sense of his bigness. He was quiet in the house and comfortable in his own bed. Frank was also pretty smart and had figured out how to open the latch on the door and would occasionally let himself quietly out for a stroll in the alley.

One day, as my roommate and I were smoking some herbal supplements and grooving on our tropical fish (Betas), there was a knock at the door. I took a quick peek out the window to see who it was and, Holy SHIT… it was the COPS!!! I stalled for a minute, yelling "Be right there!" while I frantically sprayed air freshener and my roommate did a quick clean-up of any illegal evidence. When I finally opened the door, the cop didn't appear uptight or aggressive. He smiled, introduced himself and said: "I think I have a friend of yours in my patrol car. He's been accused of theft but I thought maybe you could talk to him".

I followed the officer out to the squad car and, sure enough, there was Frank sitting in the back seat. The officer explained to me that he had gotten a call from the manager of the Kentucky Fried Chicken restaurant. Apparently a customer, who was exiting the restaurant with his freshly purchased fried chicken was assaulted by Frank. Well, Frank didn't actually assault him. He was just so big that his head was in your chest when he was on all fours. Frank just pressed his nose against this gentleman and held him to the wall until the guy gave him some of his chicken. Frank LOVED fried chicken. (Probably a good thing the guy didn't resist).

Anyway, Frank was released to my custody and the manager of KFC declined to press charges.

Then we spent the rest of the night trying to figure out how to rescue our baggy from the toilet.

CHAPTER #15

GOD is DOG—Henny Penny

Ever since my wife, Amy, and I have been together (22 years), we've always had a household mix of both dogs and cats. Although we both love, nurture and feed them, Amy would be considered the cat person and I would be dog boy.

When we met, Amy had two cats, Bilbo and Sam, and I had one dog, Chavez. Since they were all mellow, becoming housemates wasn't a big issue for them. In the ensuing years we've always had a mix of both. The upside, of course, was a continual houseful of playful, loving critters. The downside, if there is one, is that they don't live as long as humans. So in the yin and yang of life, we would usually celebrate the lives lost with a brief mourning period…and then we're off to the shelter again.

At this point I'd like to honor and praise the dedicated people who run the shelters, in particular Linda Gottwald ("Stand Up For Animals," in Marathon), from whom we have received two exceptional cats and an unforgettable dog. Linda has expanded her devotion to operate another shelter in Traverse City, Michigan, called Great Lakes Humane Society. She's also written a book called *ONCE UPON A SHELTER*. She is our patron saint of animal rescues. It's a demanding job with unlimited hours, low pay, lots of volunteerism and has its emotionally draining episodes. The mutual trait that keeps these devotees going though is their inherent love of animals (and occasionally court ordered service hours). I always have the urge to hug them to help recharge all the love they're pouring into their poor homeless charges. There's going be one huge rock-festival-style party when we all get to the "Rainbow Bridge," the fabled gathering point for deceased pets and pet-owners to reunite.

This particular story is about a beautiful little terrier mix named Penny that Amy saw in our local paper, the *Key West Citizen*. Our Florida Keys shelters, the SPCA (Society for the Prevention of Cruelty to Animals) and SUFA (Stand Up For Animals), have always run photos of animals needing adoption. Not a week goes by that Amy doesn't hand me the newspaper and say, "Aw, honey, look at this adorable face. He/she needs a home." Sometimes I try not to look, knowing what a softie I am, but it never works.

Then, of course, she showed me Penny.

I said, "Well we both have the day off. Let's take a ride over and at least give her some love."

So off we went.

For some reason, the shelter was packed that day with both adopters and adoptees. When an affable young man finally asked if he could help us, we showed him Penny's photo. He went blank for a brief moment, then said: "We're pretty busy today, and I think this particular dog needs some quiet love and private attention. She's kinda nervous. But I can show her to you real quick."

He guided us toward the rear of the shelter to an eight-foot-by-eight foot pen where Penny was running non-stop in a circular attempt to catch her tail.

"No problem," we said. "We'll come back in a day or two."

Two days later we returned to the shelter. The same gentleman was on duty.

"Remember us?" I said. "We came back to see Penny."

The young man nodded and led us to a different enclosure. When I saw Penny she had a protective cone around her neck. I said to Amy: "Oh, looks like they must have just fixed her."

The shelter staffer stuttered a bit, then said, "Take a closer look."

I've been around dogs my entire life but nothing could prepare me for what came next. Penny, out of some deep psychological urge-gone-bad, had actually caught her tail…and bit it off. The shelter veterinarian had to come in and put a few stitches in the stub end to close it up. The cone was to give it time to heal. We were stunned and there was dead silence for a minute.

The caregiver said: "I don't know what to say. She's kinda psycho and is probably going to need an awful lot of time, love and attention."

"Perfect," I said. "That's what all my teachers used to say about me too."

We came back every day for about a week to play with her and let her get to know us…and to let her heal.

When we finally took her home to meet our other dogs and cat, Penny was reclusive and would spend hours alone in the corner growling menacingly at the tail-that-once-was. When she did so, it sort of unnerved the other animals enough that they were skeptical of approaching or playing with her. Our other pets were all pretty easy-going so I kept thinking Penny would soon get over her neurosis.

We tried the dog park at Higgs Beach. It has been a place of solitude and bliss for me since I've been practicing and teaching Tai Chi there for 20-plus years. What could be better than ocean breezes, green grass, a forest of trees and lots of dogs of every shape and size? The other dogs played and ran, chasing sticks and balls for their masters, but Penny wasn't interested in other dogs or chasing anything…other than her tail.

It was the only game she knew.

We loved her like any parent would love a "special needs" child, but it was a losing battle. She'd be fine…until she wasn't, and the growling would start again. After six months, I thought we might have to seek professional help for her. The other animals sensed there was something wrong or different about her and gave her a wide berth. I began to question my own judgment. Were we not good for her? Was she not good for the other animals? We decided to just keep her safe and loved and live with the rest.

In a moment of self-doubt, I decided to seek council/wisdom from my *I-Ching Book of Changes*. I threw the ceremonial coins and referenced their response. It simply said: "Perseverance furthers."

And so it was. Penny became our "project." We paid special attention to those things that made her happy, or at least mellow. She loved car rides and would immediately jump in and sit next to me on the console of my pickup truck. There was so much constant stimulation while we were moving that I think it filled her dark shadows with light and life.

When we evacuated the Keys, due to Hurricane Irma, we drove all the way to our friends Clark and June Luster's house up in the Blue Ridge Mountains of Tennessee. Even though they live in blissful solitude on one-hundred acres at the top of a mountain, they lovingly opened their arms and house to our family of three adults, four dogs and a cat. We spent two idyllic weeks there, taking long walks, chasing butterflies, and recharging our batteries from the brutal two-day evacuation traffic jam.

Bless you Clark and June for the much appreciated hospitality.

And for the loan of the chainsaw that you knew we were going to need when we got back home.

Now the Keys were finally opening back up for returning post-storm residents, so it was time for that long ride back. The other three dogs were content to sleep in the back seat, eat and walk at rest stops. Not Penny, who was my faithful wingman for the entire trip. Who knows, maybe her initial home was with an over-the-road trucker. At any rate, she seemed happier perched up on that console watching the world go by.

When we finally returned home to the Keys we tried to keep Penny happy with other activities that she definitely enjoyed like swimming and kayaking. Since we live right on Florida Bay, we spend a lot of time in the water. She likes kayaking so much that if I pick up a paddle, even just to move it, she'll run, jump in and sit in my kayak in anticipation of an adventure. She loves to sit right behind me so I eventually had to put some bathtub no-slip strips on the hull so she'd quit slipping off when the seas got rough.

She actually loves to swim too but, unfortunately, we have a new dilemma to deal with. The North American crocodile, pushed almost to extinction by habitat encroachment, had started to rebound after dropping to as few as 200 individuals in the late 70s. A crocodile refuge was established in Key Largo and, as the crocs repopulated, they began to branch out in search of new turf (or surf as it were). Since the crocs prefer saltwater, as opposed to the freshwater gators, the Florida Keys are a great stepping stone for them to branch out. The Geiger Key Marina and Fish Camp, our favorite neighborhood tiki-bar/restaurant, sports a sign saying CAUTION—CROCODILES OBSERVED

IN AREA—USE CAUTION WHEN SWIMMING OR FISHING.

Sorry Penny. No swimming there.

Well the good news is that the North American crocodile is rather shy and reclusive. There's never been a recorded instance of one of them attacking a human. A small dog, however, would be just a perfect sized sandwich for them. So, unfortunately, our dogs are restricted to our little beach and canal and only while we're swimming with them. Just to be sure, Penny, the slowest swimmer of the dogs, has taken to riding in our inner-tubes and beach floats with us (and with a Queen-of-the-Nile countenance).

It took me awhile (DUH!) but I finally realized what all of Penny's behaviors had in common. She simply needed to sit close to us.

In the recliner, in the truck, in the kayak and even on the floats…Penny was happiest when she and I, or Amy, were attached at the hip.

Time, as they say, heals all things and eventually it became apparent that love and a forever family were all she ever needed or wanted. Penny gradually calmed down. It took a year or so but she's now so lovey-dovey that she's good with kids and plays happily with the other dogs.

Our cat even likes and trusts her now.

When I come home from work, she's the first animal licking my hands and face. A very special THANKS to Amy for seeing the love in Penny's eyes even from a grainy newspaper photo.

A word of caution though: don't EVER pet

or touch her tail stub. She gets that far-away look in her eyes and starts a low, rumbling warning growl. When that happens we just love her up and repeat the words "Only Love" until that beautiful and soulful terrier smile returns...to our loving Henny Penny.

(She's actually sitting under my desk, playing with my foot, while I write this.)

CHAPTER #16

Hold My Beer

The proper name for the art of Rope-walking is FUNAMBULISM (*fune*...French for rope, and *ambulare*...to walk in Latin).

I've been a Funambulist for 40 years, but I guess my thrill seeking really started as a rambunctious youngster like so many kids. The only thing was that the allure never ended. If it seemed like a challenge to get a thrill, I was all over it. At 73 years old now, I'm a little slower and a tad weaker but, for the most part, I'm still game. Whether it's wire-walking, skydiving, Scuba diving, dirt-biking, spelunking, hang-gliding, windsurfing, open-ocean sailing or even Everglades kayaking, the thrill and challenge are the objective for me. It's true that some of those things can be relaxing and even peaceful for a time...until they're not. Then it's Endorphin Time.

With that in mind, I guess it's finally time to answer my most asked question..."Did you ever fall or hurt yourself?" Hahahahaha (Do fish poop in the ocean?)

Well, for starters, I guess I can say none of my "mishaps" have been serious enough for me to regret what I was doing. For those of you who have shared similar experiences, I hope you've healed completely.

It's also true that not all of my challenges have been thoroughly or properly vetted but, as the saying goes: "Good decisions come from experience, and experience comes from bad decisions."

Knowing all that, you're probably wondering why I ended up being a funambulist. Fair question.

As I mentioned earlier in this book, the first time I stepped onto a tightrope, I knew instinctively that I was meant to be there. Since my background is in gymnastics it probably wasn't much of a stretch (pun not intended). Learning rope-walking or gymnastics has lots of parallels. Falling is one of them. To this day I still credit my gymnastics coach, Gaylord Hughes, with teaching me the all-important "Art of Falling." It's saved my butt more than a couple of times.

It might also be noted that as a lifelong gymnast/athlete/martial artist, I've broken every toe (phalanges, some multiple times), most of my fingers (also phalanges), hands (metacarpals, twice), feet (metatarsals, thrice) and several ribs. Add to that more burns than a barbeque and several dislocations.

Most of these mishaps occurred while I lived in Key West, but some took place while I was touring for festivals and special events. If there are bright sides to this, they would be 1) that no major bones were ever broken, and 2) I got to know lots of wonderful doctors and nurses at the emergency rooms on a first name basis.

Not all of my falls have been graceful, but none have been life-threatening and for that I thank my guardian angels, my coach Mr. Hughes and my best friend and rig-man, John Taheny. It might also be noted that "near misses" can sometimes be just as traumatic as the real thing.

My first accident that actually occurred during a performance was at an upscale hotel on the Key West waterfront. Since it was my own fault I won't name the resort, and I also don't want anyone that worked there to feel "guilty" for my own questionable decisions.

The day was warm and sunny, a Florida travelogue kind of afternoon with palm trees, mojitos and Caribbean steel drum music. I had been hired to perform poolside for a convention. I would be juggling on the tightrope for 300 well-heeled guests and the media would also be covering it.

As usual, I arrived several hours early to begin my rigging set-up. There was nothing structural near the pool to fasten my equipment to so my free-standing rig, which I had used for numerous conventions, seemed most appropriate. The rig is fabricated from black steel and resembles a hammock-stand on steroids. The rope attached to it suspended me approximately seven feet above the pool apron, which was marble tile. The only other thing below me was a steel bar (the spine of the rig) which stretched the length of the structure (approximately 12 feet) at a height of about three feet.

As I was assembling the rig, I realized that a steel ring that connected the rope to the upright was missing. Bummer. There wasn't enough time to go home or to the hardware store. I searched out the maintenance foreman and explained my plight. He said, "Let me check. I'll bet we have something that'll work."

He came back a few minutes later with an almost identical ring. It wasn't steel but it was aluminum. I was relieved and finished erecting the rig and, quickly enough, it was SHOWTIME!

Between rum-runners and sun-block, the crowd was well-oiled and ready to party. I felt strong, and the 30-minute show was fun and well-received.

Just as I finished my finale of juggling knives on the tightrope I got a huge, unwelcomed, surprise. The substitute aluminum ring suddenly snapped. It almost seemed like it happened in slow motion. One second I was balancing gracefully on the rope and then...the rope just disappeared from beneath me. As I look back it seemed very cartoonish, like something from the *ROAD RUNNER*.

I was suspended in mid-air...and then I wasn't.

Still keeping my good form, I dropped like a rock. My mind flashed to that steel bar (approximately three-feet high) directly beneath me, if I hit it with a foot, ankle or leg it wasn't going to be pretty. On the other hand, if I landed with one leg on each side of it, I might be singing falsetto.

In a desperate attempt to avoid both, I landed with one leg on each side of it...and slightly on my tiptoes.

I did manage to save the family jewels, but landing that hard on marble tile without bending my knees to compensate was too much stress on my feet and I felt a bone pop in my left foot. There was a moment of awkward silence.

Fortunately I was still standing upright when I landed, so I just looked around, smiled and took my bow.

The crowd, thinking that this was a planned, spectacular ending to the show, burst into applause.

As soon as I began to walk offstage, I knew my foot was broken. The promoter, and several patrons of my appreciative crowd, swarmed me with handshakes, congratulations and photo-ops.

I realized then that no one, except for me, knew I was injured. Someone even commented about my "creative dismount."

I was breathing measuredly, trying to disguise my pain, when the General Manager of the hotel came up and said, "Great show. I know that you've been here before but, did you know that we just redesigned our lobby? C'mon, I'll give you a little tour."

Not wanting to be discourteous, I whimpered, "Sure."

So, off we went...the manager, myself and several guests, for a *WALKING* tour of the new atrium.

I tried not to limp but the pain was definitely causing me to take short breaths. Mr. Manager noticed my labored breathing and asked me if I wanted to rest and have a drink. Of course, I thanked him, and then excused myself to go and pack my equipment. It took a concentrated effort to keep from fainting by this time.

Good thing it was my left foot because I still had to drive home. I was so embarrassed and angry with myself for trusting that aluminum coupling that, after arriving home, I downed a shot of tequila and set the bone myself.

If you've never set your own broken bone, I highly recommend an extremely stiff drink followed by some pain-killers. I felt stupid and didn't want to have to explain my bone-headed bad judgment to anyone. *Hold my beer.*

I pressed down on the angled bone, until it was straight, and then I taped it up (cast-like) and took a couple of Percocet painkillers which I had left over from a toothache. I left my homemade cast on for 10 days and then wrapped it with an Ace bandage for another two weeks. When queried, I simply told folks that it was a minor sprain.

That was 27 years ago. Today, if you see me in my flip-flops, you might notice the misshaped bone bulging slightly from the side of my left foot.

Let's just call it a "souvenir."

Interestingly enough, most accidents in Funambulism actually come from rigging failures or adverse weather conditions (wind and or rain) and have nothing to do with your balance (or lack of it).

Since most of my performances are outdoors, and up high, I have faced those challenges more than once.

The Sunset Celebration at Mallory Square in Key West is where I first developed my image on the high wire. At the time of this episode, I had been performing semi-regularly at the nightly festival for more than 30 years. I had constructed a 10-foot high, and 30-foot long tight wire that was supported by two steel A-frames. The A-frames were then attached to two existing ship cleats by nylon crane lifting straps. The tension was then provided by a two-ton hand winch called a *come-along*. The rigging was simple and strong. It was also parallel to the edge of the dock, three feet from the Gulf of Mexico, which provided me with one of the most gorgeous theater backdrops imaginable. The image of me juggling on that wire, with the world-famous Key West sunset behind me, became symbolic with the exotic allure of the Florida Keys.

It was exciting.

It was visually stimulating.

And balancing up on that wire, I was totally vulnerable to the ocean wind.

Occasionally, due to tropical weather patterns, those gentle breezes would increase to 20 knots or greater. As a windsurfer, who was accustomed to reading the wind against my body, I generally enjoyed the challenge of *Dancing with the Wind*.

Once in a great while, I would even go up and perform when the wind was as high as 20-25 knots. I loved the challenge, and so did the crowd.

But on one particular night the wind was picking up from the high 20s to 30 knots.

As I stood at the edge of the water and assessed my safety concerns, the crowd began to assemble. *NO WAY* they started to murmur. Adrenaline-junkie that I am, I suddenly became more determined and decided to "go for the Gold." You could feel the anticipation building in the crowd. *Is he really going up there in this wind?*

I mounted my rig and sat at the top for a minute to feel the wind and bolster my resolve. Now, as one of my Navy brothers loved to say, it was time to *WEED OUT THE HALF-STEPPERS.*

I rose up, took a deep breath, and took my first step. Just like when you're riding a bike, your balance is easier when you're moving. Knowing that, I kept moving steadily. My motion was consistent and my balance was challenged, but the wind seemed manageably steady...and not gusting.

But...as I neared the middle of the span I was in for a HUGE surprise (the story of my life).

The wind suddenly exploded to 40-45 knots, tropical storm strength. It was so strong that it literally lifted me off the wire!

I had been blown off the wire by smaller gusts in the past, but this was WAY above my pay grade. As I usually did when bailing out at that height, I reached out to put one hand on the cable as I was going past it. This was to slow down the top half of my body in order to make sure that my feet got underneath me. That's a must when you're 10 feet above concrete.

Unfortunately the wind was so strong that it caused me to twist slightly as I got airborne. I grabbed for the wire but by now it was slightly behind me. I got a hand on it and tried to adjust my descent.

Unfortunately, again, my shoulder didn't share that range-of-motion.

I heard a loud "POP" in my ears, and then, miraculously, I landed on my feet.

I looked out at my crowd and there was (once again) dead silence.

Having landed successfully on my feet, I was about to celebrate…until I felt a pain in my shoulder. I looked down and *HOLY CRAP!* My arm actually began about a foot lower than my shoulder. My hand was all the way to my knee. I'd never had a dislocation before, other than a finger, but there was no doubt about what had just happened.

My crowd was still silent, not knowing what to say or do. I tried to make a joke by smiling and saying, "I meant to do that" but I could feel the blood draining from my face.

I looked around and asked, "Is there a doctor in the crowd?"

Two gentlemen stepped forward and I said to them, "I heard it POP. I'm pretty sure it's not broken, but it's definitely dislocated. Do you think you can help me get it back in its socket?"

The first one said, "Sorry, but that's not my field."

The second one said, "I have some emergency room experience. If you want me to, I'll give it a try."

Not wanting to make another of my famous emergency room visits, I said "Let's go for it."

The doctor looked around and said, "I need three big guys!"

He told me to lie down on the ground and instructed them to hold me still.

By this time, Jean "Blue" Morabal, one of my fellow juggler and unicyclist performers who witnessed it all, ran up, knelt down beside me and gripped my hand to help hold my arm still. I could tell by the look on his face that he was feeling my pain. I stared into his eyes while the Doc gave my arm a good jerk. No movement...but excruciating pain. Then he told me to take a deep breath and he yanked on it again. Still nothing. On the third try, I almost blacked out. He looked at me and said, "Doesn't seem to be working, and you're looking kinda pale. I think we should get you to the hospital."

Blue helped me to my feet. I looked at my crowd and they were still in stunned silence. I must have been in shock because the rest is a bit blurry in my memory.

One of my friends ran and retrieved his truck. We called my wife, Amy, and asked her to meet us at the emergency room. She told us she was on her way. *This wasn't our first rodeo.*

Fortuitously, with some good techniques and opiates, my arm was back in place in a few hours and, with three months of intense physical therapy, I eventually regained my complete range of motion.

I did, however, get a good ribbing from Amy who said, "Honey, you're almost 70. You don't bounce as good as you used to."

I'm just happy that I still bounce at all.

And Amy, once again, had to help me get dressed for at least a month. Mirroring the emergency room visits, it was a routine that we were all too familiar with.

I can still hear my mom, who'd had hips and knees replaced, reminding me, "If you want to use that joint again, make sure you do your re-hab!"

(I did, and it worked. Thanks mom.)

The seeds of this last adventure were planted in a phone call with some of my buds in Chicago. These old neighborhood and college friends were opening a new Saloon and Garden Bar on the North Side and wanted something spectacular for their *Grand Opening.*

I told them, "Hey, I'm going to be up there visiting my folks at that time. Do you want me to come and juggle fire or something for your party?" Between some beers and Brats (Chicago's big on Bratwurst), one of them said, "Maybe we should hire you to walk between the rooftops over the Gardens." *Were they kidding?*

As you're probably getting the idea by now…I LOVE a challenge.

The Gardens were bracketed by two four-story red brick buildings.

Fastening to the roofs would put me at *five* stories. This was going to be BIG fun.

As you know, Key West was where I learned

to wire-walk but each event was a different venue presented in many different cities. This was going to be my first walk in Chicago, a city ominously nicknamed *The Windy City*. It was also where I grew up and this would also give me a chance to perform in front of (or above) lots of old friends.

Funambulism is a balancing art, but rigging for a walk is a different animal altogether. It requires a learned understanding of engineering because of the extreme tension required. Most of my high-walks were rigged, or inspected, with the help of one of my oldest friends, John (JT) Taheny, who I previously mentioned. He was a general contractor that specialized in high-rise building construction. John was a bear of a man with a heart as big as his shoulders. He had the smile of a child, the strength of Sasquatch and the loyalty of a Labrador retriever. Obviously, I trusted him with my life. I like to think he would've trusted me with his.

The brick buildings we were attaching to in this particular crossing were almost 100 years old. When the main wire is stretched more than 30-40 feet across, guy-wires are attached perpendicular to both sides of the main cable to take out the sideways slack. This particular walk was approximately 120 feet across so we used three sets of guy-wires thereby dividing the main wire into four thirty-foot sectors.

It was my first nighttime high-walk, so we were careful to rig during the daylight just to make sure everything was right. As dark skies approached, we readied the rigging for the walk. We checked the tension on the main cable and all the *guys*. As we "tuned it up," suddenly a six-inch masonry screw, that was holding one of the guy-wires, pulled right out of the ancient brittle cement and brick. With tension on the main cable at 100% on one side and 0% on the other side, the main wire was pulled into a modified Z shape.

The atmosphere went dead quiet (here we go again). I'll never forget that moment when John and I, standing nose to nose, stared at each other with sweat dripping off our chins, and realized that if I had been out on the wire just then...I wouldn't be here right now.

John looked at me and asked: "You gonna be alright? I can fix this, but I can see that you're full of adrenaline now and breathing hard."

We both knew that relaxation is key to balancing, so I said, "If you can fix your part, I think I can fix mine."

This would be the first time I ever called on my Tai Chi training in an emergency. I had always valued the Chinese martial art as a daily tonic for health and well-being, as well as a pragmatic self-defense system. This, however, was an actual challenge to my survival. My legs were shaking and I was pumping adrenaline. I walked around to the other side of the roof, shielded in the dark from the crowd by the elevator shaft, and slowly started doing some Tai Chi related breathing exercises. It took 10-15 minutes but my heart finally slowed and my hands and legs finally stopped trembling. The relaxed and deliberate breathing, blended with the balanced moves of the Yang Form, began to do their magic. I came back from stressing and thinking…to *just being.*

Now it was showtime.

John, having secured the rig, gave me a hug and then went down and came up on the opposite roof. I picked up my balance pole and stood back getting the feel of it.

Down below, the party was starting to buzz. A crowd of hundreds had spilled out into the Gardens and street and were looking skyward. It was a perfect star-lit, muggy summer night in Chi-Town. The wind, always a factor in the *Windy City,* was mild for the moment but thunderstorms were forecast for later in the evening, so time was also becoming a factor. This was also my first nighttime building-top walk. There were two major spotlights focusing on me and my wire. My white silk jumpsuit glowed against the night sky. I concentrated on long slow breaths and stepped slowly to the edge. I looked across and John gave me a thumbs up.

An interesting thing happens chemically and psychologically when you put yourself in a situation like that. Your survival instinct is your strongest instinct. The moment you step out on the wire your brain takes over and pumps opiate-like endorphins into your system. Any trepidation or nervousness you may have had is suddenly gone once you realize you have surrendered yourself. You are engulfed in a state of near intoxication where your perception, balance and focus are suddenly laser-sharp. A bomb could go off next to you and it wouldn't startle you.

It's the most peaceful dream-state I've ever experienced. One step at a time. One breath at a time. One step at a time. Breathe. Time is suspended. There is no sound. And then…BOOM!

You step onto the opposing building… and the rush you get is tantamount to an injection of a MAJOR stimulant. It feels like every pore in your body is screaming.

WHAT A RUSH!!!

And John—a bear of a man—gave me the BIGGEST bear hug.

As you can tell by my relating of this story, it was far more than just "another day at the office." It was the kind of day that John and I both lived for, nothing promised but everything to gain. Thank you, John. You may be gone physically now, but you'll always take every step with me on the high-wire. We lived to love another day. Sometimes those "near misses" make us even more alive.

Needless to say, the party that night with John and my old Chicago buds was EPIC.

The next day, I paid a visit to my folks and presented them with a video of the walk.

After that, my mom said, "Thanks for bringing the video over because I'll never be able to watch you do it live. At least if you walk in carrying a tape, I'll know that it was a success and you're okay."

You're right…I never told her.

CHAPTER #17

Diamond in the Rough

One of the things I love most about performing, particularly in outdoor venues, is the element of surprise. It's often said that spontaneity is the crown jewel of Street Performing. The weather's never the same, the crowd's never the same and, for better or worse, the show and party are never the same...and it's seldom boring.

I've been performing on the waterfront at the Mallory Square Sunset Celebration in Key West for 43 years. I've witnessed everything from Jimmy Buffett in the 70s singing and sitting on an overturned bucket, to the parade of boats arriving in the 1980 Mariel Boat Lift from Cuba. In the old days, creative giants like Tennessee Williams, Shel Silverstein and Guy Laliberte (founder of *Cirque Du Soleil*) mixed anonymously with bar owners (Capt. Tony Tarracino), politicians, fishermen, hippies and Key West locals, fondly referred to as "Conchs." (There were also a few smugglers in the mix, but that's a subject for another book.) It was a collective consciousness. They gathered there to commune with their neighbors, to say goodbye to the sun, and hello to the evening. There were no vendors in that era, so everyone brought their own libations or recreational medication. Then they picked a spot at the edge of the pier where they could dangle their legs over the water and waited for God's light show to begin.

Nowadays, people head for the bars shortly after sunset, but in the old days that was when the tempo started picking up. People would skinny-dip off the seawall in the deep blue waters of the Florida Bay ship channel. The strong tidal currents made it both refreshing and challenging. As the last orange glow disappeared in the west, the swimmers started climbing back up onto the pier just as the drummers began to congregate near mid-pier. The drummers were the heartbeat of the sunset celebration. Some bongo players were Cuban, while the Puerto Ricans played congas and the Africans jammed on their djembes. The Caribbean rhythms were like a cultural drug.

And dancing bordered on the orgasmic.

Inevitably, as in all good tropical parties, out came the Limbo stick. Some of the swimmers were actually still naked while doing the Limbo. There were no tourists back then so it didn't matter, ergo anyone to offend. Every single person found something acoustic to add to the beat whether it was a drum or two beer bottles and a garbage can. And, when the drummers began the old Calypso call-and-response songs, EVERYONE did the responses. I can almost still hear them singing *"DAY-O"* and *"WHO PUT THE PEPPER IN THE VASELINE?"* The music was tribal and ancient and sweaty. The party usually lasted well into the hot, humid nights. This was at a time in our history when the sexual revolution cross pollinated with the drug revolution and the result was titillating. A popular quote that resonated was..."We're all here, because we're not all there!" This was a party that was too good to go undiscovered. It bordered on magic.

What started as an unscripted gathering of like-minded sunset worshippers, gradually morphed into an internationally known daily celebration. Now, 40 years later, the nightly festival features top-tier busking shows from around the world, dozens of unique and original artists and local foods prepared on site. Oh, yes, and the crowd has grown from the hundreds to the thousands but, as middle-class America discovered it, the character of the event and the characters who exemplified it became distinctly more conservative. Tourism was the new buzz-word in Key West and the Tourist Commission frowned on naked-dancing, pot-smoking and public sex. Go figure. In spite of its evolution though, the Sunset Celebration still remains a place where surprises and magic seem to be the norm.

People don't necessarily come to dance, sing and swim anymore...but they definitely keep coming. Now they come to enjoy the shows, patronize the artists and food vendors, and take selfies with one of America's most stunning sunsets over the Gulf of Mexico. It was one of those chamber-of-commerce picture-perfect evenings when this story unfolded.

I came to Mallory Square in the late afternoon one day to prepare for a tight-wire performance scheduled to begin immediately after sunset. It was a gorgeous Florida sky with towering thunderheads and light breezes from the west. It generally took me close to an hour to erect the A-frames that supported my cable and to get the tension just right, so I needed to safely secure everything before the crowds arrived. The rig was approximately 10-feet high, 22-feet long and only 3 feet from the water's edge, so my crowd would be a semi-circle facing the sun. I normally would put down some strips of Astro-turf for the front row to sit on. The faux grass was not only for my audiences comfort but also to delineate a safety zone so that my fire-and-knife juggling on the wire wouldn't endanger anyone that ventured too close. The only person allowed in that stage area would be a volunteer that I would pick to help me climb up to the wire. I, of course, was fully capable of mounting the rig myself, but I'd use an unwitting tourist to create a comedy routine that was part-slapstick and part vaudeville.

As the crowd trickled in and grabbed their spots on the rugs, I puttered about, laying out the rest of my juggling equipment. This day's crowd was an interesting mix of American north-easterners, Asian and European tourists. An interesting socioeconomic blend. Families with kids and couples with cocktails began to congregate in my front row. The kids sitting in front were enthralled by a wild

116

chicken and her little chicks having a buffet of someone's spilled popcorn. In my peripheral vision I became aware of a woman standing next to my rig and looking down at the ground. She seemed to be searching or scanning for something. I walked over to her and asked, "Hi, did you lose something?" She looked up at me and broke into tears. She didn't answer me but instead continued crying and continued her search.

She was totally overwrought. As I groped for something appropriate to say, a gentleman approached me. He wasn't emotional, but he looked a little sad.

"Do you recognize her?" he said quietly. "She's my wife, and she was your volunteer who helped you up on the wire in your show last night. She had her hair braided last night and it's brushed out today so she looks a little different."

When he said that, I did remember them both. I had pegged them as upwardly mobile from the northeast. Maybe Connecticut, well-dressed and well-spoken. I said, "I don't want to pry but is she going to be okay? And what's she looking for?"

"Well, let me explain what happened," he said. "When we left your show last night at Mallory we walked over to the Bagatelle Restaurant on Duval Street. While we were eating, my wife Angie looked down and the two-and-a-half carat diamond in her wedding ring was missing. We're talking $40,000 worth. The restaurant staff was very helpful and joined us to search the entire room. Nothing. So we traced our steps back to Mallory because she

117

remembered it was still in its setting when she was here."

Oh No! I thought to myself. *I hope they don't have any misplaced suspicions that I'm involved in the disappearance of her diamond.*

I approached the young lady and told her how sorry I was to hear what had happened and wished her luck in her search. Then I said "Look, I'm not starting my show for another 10-15 minutes. Why don't we ask a few folks to help us scour the area?"

Truth be told, it had been 24 hours since the stone went missing, so I wasn't feeling too optimistic, but…nothing ventured, nothing gained.

We deputized a few friends and then spread out to work off an imaginary grid. The deck of the pier was a coral-colored concrete mixed with sections of red brick which made a visual sighting even more improbable. As we crawled around on our hands and knees the sun began to sink into Florida Bay and I could see the look of resignation in Angie's eyes. The light would soon fade and so would the hope of a happy ending.

I wanted to say something to make Angie feel better but couldn't find the right words. Then, as I finished wiping the sweat off my glasses, I put them back on and happened to look down. The last ray of light from the setting sun made something catch the corner of my eye. It made a glancing sparkle as it reflected the sunlight. I got down on one knee and took one more peek…and there it was. The prettiest diamond I've ever seen.

"Angie!!" I screamed. "Bonanza!"

The stone had been pressed down into the soft expansion-joint that separates the sections of concrete. Someone had probably stepped on it and unknowingly ground it in. I looked up and Angie's tears of loss suddenly turned into tears of joy, and her husband was smiling like a lottery winner. They both gave me a huge hug. Hallelujah!

And just in time... it was SHOWTIME! I gave Angie another hug and high-fived her husband, Jay. I was pumped now and this was going to be fun.

After a rousing and newly-inspired show the three of us walked over to Meson de Pepe's Bar and had mojitos. They tipped me $100, but it was the priceless look on Angie's face that was the real treasure that day.

Angie and Jay come down almost every year now to vacation in Key West and every time they do, they tip me $100 and we drink a mojito to toast our luck and our friendship.

And I never fail to compliment Angie on her dazzling diamond ring.

Through all the years at the Sunset Celebration, the magic still continues in so many different ways. (And, yes, sometimes late at night, when everyone's gone, I still occasionally skinny-dip.)

CHAPTER #18

Bad News, Good News

It's true that I appear to have a Guardian Angel watching over me. I don't know that I've ever done anything to deserve it but, nonetheless, I've been lucky, or fortunate, more often than not. Many of these stories relive joys, chuckles, some near-misses and interesting twists of fortune.

The next narrative is more difficult for me because of the pain, both mental and physical, that was involved. It deals with fate, gratitude and an alarm call to everyone.

This tale starts out in the early 90s. The wild abandonment of the 60s, 70s and 80s drug-and-sexual revolutions had evolved into a troubling hangover of drug abuse and sexually transmitted diseases. The wild parties (read: drug-fueled orgies) were being replaced by Rehabilitation Clinics and County Health Programs.

Unlimited, unmonitored and untested drug production was resulting in record overdose deaths, and sexually transmitted diseases were no longer cured with a shot of penicillin—and a national health crisis developed. Actually it was a global problem but, since this is personally anecdotal, I'll be more locally specific.

The Human Immunodeficiency Virus (HIV-1) can severely damage your immune system and ultimately lead to Acquired Immune Deficiency Syndrome (AIDS). Thought to have originated in Africa in approximately 1920, the first diagnosed cases of the virus in the U.S. were sometime around 1981. Between then and 2016, an estimated 675,000 people in America died from the disease. It was a huge and growing concern and, in small towns like Key West where everyone knows everyone, it was deeply personal.

Local community non-profit health clinics, along with county health departments, were beseeching everyone to come in and get free blood testing. The means of transmission were not even clear. Blood transfers, either from sex or transfusions were suspected. Unfortunately, too many people in our small island were being affected, either personally or through family experiences. Most everyone I knew was now getting tested annually.

One of my best friends, who recently had undergone major surgery, asked me if I wanted to join him when he went for his blood testing. A local clinic was offering it for free every Tuesday morning so joining him was a no-brainer. *Better to be safe than sorry.*

We biked on over to the lab and signed up.

The folks there were very courteous and helpful. They asked us if we'd like our blood samples tested for all common viruses. *Yes,* again a no-brainer.

It wasn't crowded at all and we chatted with the receptionist while we waited for our results.

After 30 minutes, a doctor came out and gave my friend the good news he was hoping for. In spite of several blood donations, his test came back negative for HIV.

Then he turned to me and said "Well, the good news is that your HIV test results also came back negative...but the bad news is that you tested positive for Hepatitis-C."

There was an awkward silence for a moment. I didn't know exactly what that entailed and he suddenly appeared to be rather uneasy about specifics. I glanced at my friend and then back at the doctor with that unspoken question-mark look on my face.

The doctor sighed and then started slowly: "Well, it's a virus that we don't know much about. It attacks the liver, and there's currently no known cure for it. The good news is that, if you stop drinking alcohol today, you could still live another good 5-10 years."

He recommended I stop back at a later date to get some dietary suggestions from him and then shook my hand and we left.

Wait. WHAT??? On the bike ride home I tried my best to digest this new revelation. *He didn't really say that did he? That can't be right. I feel fine. Shit, I'm only 47 years old! Maybe it was just a false positive test.*

Maybe this was from uncontrolled drug use in the 70s and 80s? Maybe they'll find a cure. Maybe, maybe...maybe.

I pedaled and prayed.

This was 1993 and I didn't have a smart phone, Google, or Alexa in those days, so I had to really dig to find out any information about this virus that I'd been hearing about but not paying much attention to. No one could actually even agree about how it was transmitted and even the treatment was speculative.

I consulted with anyone that I thought was medically educated. Although there wasn't a lot of information available, it did seem to be spreading rapidly amongst the Boomer generation (born between 1944-1964). Hepatitis-C related deaths were under the radar but were climbing rapidly.

Obviously, the first thing I did was to stop drinking alcohol. I didn't consider myself an alcoholic but I was definitely drinking regularly in those days. Beer, Tequila and Grand Marnier. Enough to make me dance better, but not enough to fall down. I love live music and the bars are where the bands play, so sobriety was a challenge. I switched to soda water and colas and, when I needed something a little more, I smoked pot.

The results were immediately apparent. No more hangovers and better overall health and vitality. Since I was aggressively practicing and training for my Black Belt testing in TaeKwonDo at the time, this newly disciplined physical approach provided welcome returns.

The challenge of martial arts gave me

something positive to focus on. I didn't want to dwell on the obvious problem so I threw myself into training. It kept me occupied and preoccupied.

It was a few short years later, in early 1996, when I met my soul mate, Amy Meshew.

She showed up one night at the Mallory Square Sunset Celebration right after my performance. Cute, pert, sexy and saucy, she just walked up, sat down and spoke to me like an old friend. I guessed that, because of her apparent familiarity, I must have met her before. I asked, "Have you ever seen my show before?"

She laughed and said, "Haha, I've been watching you since I was 13-years old."

She was then 32 and I was 49, 17 years her senior. I briefly considered the age gap...and then immediately dismissed it. As we talked it became obvious that our attitudes, philosophies and sense of humor had an uncanny amount of parallels.

We decided to meet the next day for café con leche. It didn't take long for those warm feelings to ignite. We fell in heat, and then in love. Before long we were spending almost every day together.

I explained my Hep-C diagnosis to Amy and she empathized. She was aboard for whatever challenges or complications that might ensue. As of this writing, we're now in the 24th year of our relationship and thankfully, after annual blood testing, she's never shown any signs of the virus.

Later that year, as I turned 50 years old, I received my 1st Degree Black Belt and life was sweet. Encouraged and supported by Amy, I went on to enjoy several years of regional competitions, continuing education and eventually teaching.

To no one's surprise, except for her mother's, Amy and I were married on August 23rd, 1998, at the Audubon Gardens on Whitehead Street in old town Key West. My best friend, Barry Kaiser, came from New Orleans to be my best man and Amy's niece, Jamie Meshew, came from Savannah to be her bridesmaid. We were married by the Key West Police Chaplain and our Pastor and friend, Steve Torrence.

The Audubon Gardens were lush and tropical. It was a veritable jungle of vines, flowers, palm trees and friends. The perfect place for an island wedding. Also the perfect place for a jungle rain. Immediately after the ceremony there was a huge clap of thunder and then, it started POURING. Even that actually felt like a good omen and we laughed and danced in the rain (fortunately, the band was on the covered porch).

As five years slid by I was buoyed by the fact that I had displayed no apparent symptoms from the Hep-C virus and I also started hearing about experimental treatments like Interferon. One of my old Navy buddies, also a Hep-C patient, told me he had just finished Interferon treatments and that the cure was worse than the disease. He said it made him feel weak and nauseous, although the virus was now practically negligible. He had been treated at his local Veterans Administration Hospital.

I had mixed feelings. I still didn't really feel sick and the thought of getting nauseous because of the medication wasn't very appealing to me. I was beginning to hear about medicines with practically no side effects, but they weren't available through the Veterans Administration and, without insurance, they were prohibitively expensive ($110,000).

The good news was that it was now almost 10 year since my diagnosis. The bad news was that I started showing symptoms: I was lethargic. More and more I constantly felt exhausted. Not only was I losing my stamina but, after even the slightest exertion, I'd have to take a rest or a nap. Amy, now my wife, started to notice that my eyes were slightly jaundiced when I was overly fatigued.

Over the next six-to-eight years it grew progressively worse. Fortunately treatment inroads were being made and the cost of the medications was coming down. Unfortunately, even at $50,000-$80,000, it was still out-of-reach for me.

Hepatitis C is a strange disease. There was no pain, and relatively few outward symptoms, other than the overwhelming torpor. With the exception of Amy, hardly anyone knew that I was sick. When I felt overcome and depleted I simply stayed in bed. No one ever really saw me "sick." I only went out when I felt nearly-normal, and those days were beginning to get fewer and far between.

When I pushed myself to perform my show, I'd become so tired I'd have to go to bed for two days. This was now becoming a serious problem. I couldn't carry my weight financially due to my physical inertia, and Amy was gradually shouldering more and more of the fiscal burden. Not carrying my share of the load was also throwing me into a depressive funk.

Then one day I woke up with some serious internal pain. It was in the area of the kidneys. I kept hoping it was something minor and would just pass, but it quickly got worse.

Amy took one look at me. "C'mon. I'm taking you to the hospital."

I thought *Maybe it's just a kidney stone.*

When we got to the Emergency Room, I could barely walk from the pain. I was thrilled when they immediately accepted my newly-acquired Medicare Card (Thank you Lord and Medicare).

After beaucoup questions and tests, kidney stones were ruled out, but no definitive diagnosis could be made, so they gave me some strong pain meds and sent me home. They said to come back if anything changed. That was Friday afternoon and by Monday morning the pain was getting worse, and something did change. While I was a putting on my shirt Amy said, "Wow. What's that rash on your side?"

By the time we got back to the hospital the pain was almost unbearable. I practically crawled on my knees into the Emergency Room. The doctor looked at my eyes, then looked at my rash and said, "That's one mean case of shingles you've got. We're going to admit you."

With that said, he administered a shot of enough opiates to let me exhale again and they wheeled me away.

Since my active hepatitis virus had already

weakened my immune system, the case of shingles intensified so severely that I spent a full week in the Lower Keys Medical Center.

Shingles is caused by the same virus responsible for chickenpox. *WHAT'S THE DEAL WITH ALL THESE VIRUSES?* It took a full month for the rash to run its course, but the toll it took on me was debilitating. I was getting weaker and weaker. The shingles seemed to have aggravated the Hep-C virus. After that, and for the next two years, my condition deteriorated. No pain, but NO energy and eventually NOT MUCH WORK.

And I was slipping into the depths of depression.

One day Amy and I had just finished practicing Tai Chi on the White Street Pier in the hope that it would bolster my compromised immune system, when Amy said, "Why don't you go see Dr. Wagstaff and see what he says?" Made sense, so off I went to Key West Urgent Care and Dr. Brian Wagstaff.

I liked and trusted Dr. Brian. I had just started seeing him and he seemed extremely capable and knowledgeable. He listened to me and said, "Well let's just start out with a complete blood workup and see what that tells us."

A few days later I went in for the results. Dr. Brian, and his positive attitude, always made me feel comfortable. That day was no different. He read me the whole list of results and interpreted them for me. Heart...excellent. Lungs...fine. Kidneys...check. Blood pressure...normal, etc.

"You're actually in great shape," he said. "Except for your Hep-C. Your viral load is through the roof."

"I kinda figured," I said.

"Have you considered any options to deal with this?"

"Well, I'm hearing about new cures, but I haven't got an extra $80,000 laying around and the Veterans Administration is not approving me for any of those treatments."

"Look," he said, "I know a doctor who specializes in viruses." With that, he scribbled down a name and number for me, and said, "Give him a call. It can't hurt to ask."

It turns out this doctor, I'll call him Dr. G, was with our local Monroe County Health Department. They're right in town at the Old Gato Building on Simonton Street. I called and made an appointment.

When I went in, Dr. G, and his unassuming and congenial nurse Nikki, immediately made me feel at ease. Of course there were a lot of questions and consent forms. They wanted to know all of my symptoms and medical history. Dr. G explained to me that there were several non-profit patient assistance programs that worked to pair patients with appropriate pharmaceutical trials involving prospective cures. He asked if I was willing to take a myriad of tests and then to share that test information with these companies. If I were accepted into the trials, the medications would be *GRATIS!*

He wasn't kidding about "quite a few tests." I began a semi-weekly battery of blood tests, MRIs, EKGs, ultra-sounds, a colonoscopy and more. Dr. G also reminded me regularly that recreational street drugs were not my friend, and that any progress I made through a pharmaceutical trial would be lost if I violated my pledge to remain "drug-and-alcohol-free." I could see by the pain in his face that not everyone had finished the program successfully. I vowed to myself to remain focused.

After four months of probing and prodding, I finally received a call from a Patients Assistance Program that had paired me with a Pharmaceutical Company. The caller essentially said, "Congratulations. Your testing results (and appropriate viral genome) have made you suitable for our Hepatitis-C trial program. If you agree to the terms and conditions of the program we'll begin shipping you 90 days of medication. FREE OF CHARGE."

Pinch me!!!

I was overjoyed to be a medical guinea pig, and guardedly optimistic about my chances for recovery. The drug being administered was called Epclusa, and the preliminary studies had shown it to be overwhelmingly effective. I got my first shipment via Overnight Mail the next day. At that time, the cost for a 30 day supply of tablets was slightly more than $26,000.

It was as if someone had just handed me nearly $80,000.

The instructions were simple but demanding.

They said that one tablet MUST be taken every day WITHOUT A MISS. If one day was missed, the entire regimen would have to start over again at the beginning. I immediately put an oversized calendar on my wall and checked it off every morning when I medicated.

The weekly blood tests continued and every week Doctor G would read me my new results. My viral load, which began at a skyrocketing count of 7 million, lowered slowly to 3 million and then shrunk weekly into the thousands. One day, 2 months into the program, I was starting to feel more energetic. I told Doctor G this and he smiled at me and said, "Your count this week is down to 14."

I laughed, and asked, "You mean 14 thousand?"

"No. Just 14."

I was feeling peppy and optimistic for the first time in a very long time. By the time I finished the 90-day program (with NO side effects) the virus was no longer detectable in my system. I was waking up feeling strong and began taking on a full load of activities again. I got the spring back in my step and felt like I had gotten back 25 years of missing spunk.

It was a gift from heaven for Amy and me both. I was back to full-time performances and carrying my weight with household duties again. And just in the nick of time…

One month later Hurricane Irma, a category 5 storm, took aim at Key West and the Lower Florida Keys.

We had ridden out category 1 and 2 storms

before but this was a monster. After Hurricane Andrew (Cat 5) struck Miami in 1992, I'd seen the utter destruction a Cat 5 storm could do. *NO WAY JOSÉ* were we staying. We packed my Toyota Tundra and Amy's Prius with four dogs, one cat, my rig-man Danny Reed, and a kayak trailer loaded with our favorite boats. Thus began a 2,200 mile (3 week) evacuation odyssey to the safety of our friends, Clark and June Lusters, mountain-top home in Tennessee. That trip alone is worthy of its own chapter (soon to come).

The point is that, after we returned to the Hurricane Irma aftermath and damage in the Keys, I joined in with my neighbors to man chainsaws and do stump-removal from sunrise to sunset for almost 6 weeks. I felt like Superman. I had my strength and stamina back and my mojo rejuvenated.

None of that would have been possible without the Epclusa, without the Pharmaceutical company, without the Patient Assistance Program, without Dr. G and Nurse Nikki, without Dr. Wagstaff and without Amy.

When I asked Dr. G if I could use his (and Nurse Nikki's) full name to thank them for the incredible gift of health they steered me towards, he said, "A thank you is not necessary, Will. This is our job and we're happy to do it. We're all a team here. All your information will remain confidential and, as a team, we're grateful for your positive results."

I can't thank everyone enough that helped me and, yes, Doctors Wagstaff and G are still monitoring my progress. In my world, they are

Angels.

So my message in all of this is for everyone to PLEASE GET TESTED, whether you have symptoms or not. And don't give up if you test positive and can't afford the medication. Keep asking and searching because there's more help out there than most of us know about, and who knows, it could save your life. It certainly gave me back the quality of mine.

ADDENDUM: When I was first diagnosed with Hep-C in the early 90s, there was no known cure for the virus. Since then, several different medications have attained successful cure rates in the high 90% range. As I sit and write this, it is December 1st, World AIDS Day. Since the start of the epidemic, 32 million people worldwide have died from AIDS-related illnesses. There is still no cure, but treatment options are improving.

CHAPTER #19

KAHM SAHM NEE-DA
(Korean for Thank You)

In 1970, I was studying Art & Design at Southern Illinois University in Carbondale, Illinois. I had been honorably discharged from the Navy three years earlier and was receiving educational funding assistance from both the Illinois Veterans' Grant Program and the Federal Military College Assistance Program (G.I. Bill).

Although I had spent most of my Navy hitch in the Atlantic fleet, I was now classmates with many returning veterans from the Vietnam Conflict. So many of them had experienced the horrors of war and were reluctant to talk about it.

However, the two subjects that most of them did talk freely and often about were drugs and martial arts.

The appeal of drugs was understandable. Access to marijuana and opiates in southeast Asia was widespread, and the terror of combat combined with the loss of comrades begged for self-medication. It was with those fellow veterans that I first experimented with recreational drugs.

Simultaneously, there was also a burgeoning interest in the martial arts. Many servicemen (and servicewomen), stationed in Asia, were getting their first glimpse into Asian fighting techniques. There was Karate from Japan, Taekwondo from Korea, Kung Fu and Tai Chi from China, Kickboxing from Thailand and Kali stick-fighting from the Philippines just to name a few.

These ancient disciplines, once closed to westerners, were suddenly enjoying increased exposure by the popularity of a string of successful Bruce Lee Kung Fu movies.

My introduction to the martial arts began in that college setting. I would attend training classes three times a week in a local park where a Vietnam Vet, appropriately named Karate Al, would school us in the most basic Karate moves. He had studied and trained while stationed in Japan.

Karate Al was Caucasian. He came from a big family of brawling Irish brothers. His style was considered brutish but effective. I almost walked out of the first class until I comprehended his philosophy. He would start the class by walking down the row of students and indiscriminately slap the bejeezus out of some unsuspecting recruit.

Each newbie that was assaulted responded with the same look of surprise and anger. No one was brave enough or stupid enough to challenge him. Then he would bow to you.

The first time he did it to me the blow turned

my head sideways. I was pissed, but tried not to show it. I didn't want him to know I was offended or aggravated.

The next couple of times he struck me were just as hard, but had lost the element of surprise. After a few more times I realized that not only was I not shocked by it, but I began to understand that it wasn't really all that painful...just startling.

Finally, one day when he whacked me a good one, I absorbed his blow without ever losing eye contact with him. He smiled, bowed...and then shook my hand.

It was my first testing of sorts. It was simple. The first *one second* of combat is very often the most important. If you are distracted either physically, psychologically, or emotionally by the shock of an attack, then you have lost that all-important first second to respond.

This, of course, is not a teaching method that would translate well in a general self-defense class or family dojo, but I can guarantee it's effective. It was also my first realization that martial arts were as psychological as they were physical.

I only had a nine-month window to train with Mr. Karate Al before he finished school and moved on, but I can remember almost everything he taught me. With Karate Al, it paid to pay attention.

Fast forward ten years to a beach in Key West. As I was enjoying the life of a windsurfing beach bum, I would spend six-to-seven days a week sailing off South Beach with other "board-heads" and beach-bunnies.

Just after sunrise each morning, I would wake up from the gypsy rooster crowing just outside my window. Like most Key West chickens he had no internal clock, so he actually crowed at all hours of the day and night. I could relate.

I'd get up, make my cafe con leche, twist a joint, jump on my bicycle and head down to the beach. There were racks at the beach where we could lock our gear so we'd spend most of the day, on site, sunning and sailing.

The summer wind was usually calmer in the morning and so it was a good time to repair equipment and trade adventures stories from the night before with the other salty dogs.

One morning, when I got to the beach, I saw a gentleman doing Tai Chi on a deck near the water. Tai Chi is a form of Chinese Kung Fu that's practiced slowly and gracefully. It was peaceful and beautiful to watch. He seemed so in-tune with nature. His movements reflected the ebb and flow of the waves, while his hands seemed to shape the wind. Each action had its own corresponding breathing technique.

Kung Fu, on the other hand (respectful pun intended), employs similar moves and strategies but is instead practiced with speed and power.

One day, I finally introduced myself to the gentleman and complimented him on his form and, wouldn't you know it, his name was "Tai Chi Norm." He was handsome, personable and entertaining.

"You're welcome to work out with me if

you'd like," he offered.

Gradually, over time, 10-12 other folks joined us to work out at the southern end of Duval Street. Nothing formal. Just a loose group of tie-dyed long-hairs, both male and female, living the sandals life. An old concrete deck made the Tai Chi movements a lot easier than being in the sand.

It was an informal teacher-student relationship that lasted five-to-six years as we bonded over martial arts and sun-worshipping.

There's no governing organization associated with Tai Chi, as there is with most martial arts, so there are no belts or seniority levels. There are, of course, old school Grand Masters that are revered for their expertise, but most everyone else is just different levels of students on their own personal paths.

Norm eventually moved on from Key West, but I'll always treasure his friendship and zen-ship. He opened a valuable door for me.

I've studied/practiced with several different Tai Chi adherents over the years, and each one had a different style and something new to be learned.

One of my favorite lessons was with one of my favorite teachers...in one of my favorite places.

Bayview Park, on Truman Avenue in Key West, is a cute little one-block of grass, trees, tennis and basketball courts, monuments, and SPACE. Fairly underutilized, the peace and quiet there lent itself to relaxing endeavors. This exact park was where I had learned to walk the tightrope.

It was also where I found Lydia Wong. Lydia

shared my fondness for Bayview Park and I would see her there leading several students in the Tai Chi Yang form. Ms. Wong, a native of Singapore, was small in stature but enormous in spirit, the embodiment of Qi flow. Her enjoyable teaching style was less about perfection and more about feeling good, embracing joy, moving with ease and releasing stress with a marriage of breathing and balance. Once again, I knew that I had discovered someone that I was honored to learn from. It wasn't long before I joined her. It was also during these sessions that I realized that martial arts and rope-walking were cut from the same cloth. *Balance, Breath, Focus and efficiency of Movement.*

One spring morning, after practicing our forms, I watched Ms. Wong take something from her equipment bag and begin one of the most beautiful of all martial arts routines—the Tai Chi Sword Form.

The air was sweet and still. The flowering red royal Poinciana trees were a perfect tropical stage drop for this centuries-old Asian discipline as she quietly bowed and began. Her movements seemed like classical music. She danced and lunged, parried and thrust. I swear, even the birds stopped singing to watch her. And a smothering blanket of humidity slowed both time and movement, and the rest of the world faded into the background.

I was enthralled.

Thus began my educational journey into the Sword Form. It didn't take me long to realize that the movement that Ms. Wong executed looked so effortless, was anything but. This was a demanding discipline, and performing it outdoors in the tropics was a physical challenge, but like all good teachers, inspiration (and perspiration) by example ruled the day. We practiced until the sweat was running off our faces in rivulets. It took most of a year to even begin to feel comfortable with this challenging routine but, even then, I felt like a hippo next to the grace and lightness of Ms. Wong's effortless movements. Finally, just as I was starting to feel more accomplished, unfortunately for me, it was time for Ms. Lydia to move on to another adventure in another time zone.

I look back fondly on those days...and still keep in touch with Lydia Wong, who now lives and teaches in hauntingly picturesque San Miguel de Allende, Mexico. Although I certainly miss her guidance and presence, she still resides in both my heart and mind. In keeping with the times, we still communicate through Facebook.

Another teacher, another style and another martial arts experience. I'm indebted to every one of my teachers for each piece of the puzzle that is me. I am also them.

Time flies though, and so does change, and alarmingly, I began to lose my focus. My life seemed to be going "off the rails," as they say, and there was a cold wind blowing some bad juju into my life.

As the 80s turned to the 90s, I began to succumb to the allure of the Key West night life. My beach and Tai Chi days began morphing into partying club nights and, within one short year, I was closing the bars and running with the "night crawlers." My energy producing sun was giving way to an ominously dark moon. Key West, in those days, was a dangerous place to let your guard down. The temptations were treacherous and the access was perilously easy. It wasn't long before I started using pharmaceutical help to run with the big dogs.

Cocaine is a fickle mistress. It can take you to the top of a mountain, only to push you off when you run out. So many people were experimenting with this insidious drug that it was in danger of becoming normalized. There was so much inexpensive and high-quality blow in Key West in those days that it was actually difficult to avoid it. Weekend flings soon turned into daily consumption. I was using it to stimulate myself for my performances and then more of it to enhance my social life. Ironically, the drug that I was using to be more social began to make me more solitary. I went from listening to music in bars, to listening to music at home, to hearing my own music in my head, and some of my "real" friends were beginning to ring my alarm bells.

Many of the fishermen-turned-marijuana-smugglers were now coming back from Columbia with a new product. We called it Columbian Pink. It was coke so pure that when you opened the sealed packages you could smell it from across the room. The purity was both exciting and terrifying. You could have either the high of your life...or the high of your death. No joke.

I was living alone and had no pets, dogs or

cats at the time and hadn't met Amy yet, so I had few restrictions or commitments...ergo, no one to help me reflect morally.

Like any intoxicant, whether it be alcohol or drugs, there is a tipping point where it ceases to be fun and begins to be a problem. It finally occurred to me that I had not only passed that point, but so had several of my friends. My spare time was spent daydreaming about my next high. More and more of my friends and activities were drug-related.

I knew that I needed to quit and focus on my mental and physical health but, after each week-long cleansing and fasting, I would eventually relapse...and call my dealer. It was just too easy in those days and, if he didn't answer, there was always another coke merchant somewhere nearby. One phone call and whatever you desired would be delivered to your door in 20 minutes by moped.

All my life I've loved music and, as I've mentioned above, the music was in the bars, so I'd eventually end up doing the Duval Crawl but, after the first drink or two breaking down my resolve, I started looking for the pay phone and digging in my pockets to see how much money I had on me.

Sometimes, when you can't get hold of a dealer, you let your guard down and the need to feel that unique euphoria pushes you to make bad choices and do stupid things...like approach shady strangers in shady places. You take chances and you know it's dangerous, but the danger, the hunt, the kill of the score, becomes a high unto itself. I found myself in places I didn't want to be, doing things I didn't want to admit.

I kept trying to quit…and kept failing. Finally, knowing that I needed some outside help, I made an appointment with the local county mental health clinic.

Asking for help, when you consider yourself to be self-reliant and in-charge, isn't all that easy. I went in with a head full of anxiety and trepidation.

The people at the clinic were helpful and efficient. The wait wasn't long and their attitudes were non-judgmental and supportive.

Before long, I was introduced to my counselor. A personable and professional gentleman in his forties. Obviously, information shared there is confidential, so I can't name my doctor, but I will always be grateful to him. Of course, the first thing he advised was to stay out of the places where coke flourished. *Wait, these were my favorite bars*, I thought.

Suck it up Buttercup. Are you serious about quitting?

The second thing Dr. Counselor instilled in me was to not feel stigmatized and to start loving myself again. His next most important lesson for healing was *TRY EVERYTHING*.

"Whether the methods are meditation, Alcoholics Anonymous, Narcotics Anonymous or simple group therapy, try it all. Not everything will be your cup of tea, but try them all.

"Just like a journeyman, the more tools you have in your bag, the more options you have to repair things."

After several months (and soul-destroying relapses), I began to show progress and was assigned to an "early recovery group" of people my age. Knowing that other people are experiencing similar challenges also adds to your strength, resolve and empathy. I traded rueful stories with fishermen, housewives, bar owners, and lawyers…all suffering the same pitfalls and depressing failures.

It was during these group sessions that I finally had an epiphany. I was trying to end a bad habit…without replacing it with good one. As someone with an addictive personality, that made simple and obvious sense to me. Even though I wasn't exactly sure of what I wanted to pursue to fill my empty space, I put my antennae up for something enjoyable, challenging and positive.

One day, as I was doing my laundry with a work-out friend of mine in a small strip mall named Havana Plaza on Flagler Avenue, we walked down the line of shops to a small unit on the end with an ATA sign in the window.

Inside was a tiny dojang, a Korean School for Taekwondo, offered by the American Taekwondo Association.

A children's class was just getting out and some adults in traditional Korean Dobuks (martial arts uniforms) were arriving for the next class.

I immediately noticed that all the departing and arriving students were bowing and removing or donning their shoes at the edges of the matted work-out floor. The Black Belt instructor (Sabum) was bowing and shaking hands with everyone at the door.

This was obviously not like one of Karate Al's

classes. This was a *traditional* Korean dojang where greetings and commands were all done in Korean…even for the kids.

I was impressed.

Over the next few weeks, I slid by occasionally to peek in the window to watch the sessions and suss the character of the school itself. There was no talking amongst students and anyone not actually performing was standing at attention, yet they all seemed happy and focused.

I had been working out by lifting weights at home every other day for months with my friend, Mauricia Malpica, one of the artists from Mallory Square. He was from Argentina and, like myself, also had an athletic background. We had an energizing hour routine with free weights and lots of bad jokes. We'd been discussing expanding our work-outs to include something more challenging. *Could this be it?*

One day, during a five-minute break in the class, the head instructor and school owner, Mr. Bob Lilly, stepped outside, said hello and introduced himself. His manner was a bit of a conundrum. He was friendly but formal. Rigid but flexible. Imposing but welcoming. He asked if we were interested in participating.

In my head I heard my counselor say *TRY EVERYTHING!* I thought *Why not?*

The adult classes that best fit our schedule were on Monday, Wednesday and Friday at noon for an hour. The $40 per month was reasonable and the first dobuk was free. Sparring equipment would eventually cost an extra hundred bucks but, to anyone who made it that far, the cost was well worth it. The classes consisted of several dozen men and women, from 16 to 76 years old, in all levels of expertise.

I would soon learn, to my dismay, that midday workouts in full-length uniforms made of heavy cotton (in the tropics) in a studio with NO air conditioning was the first challenge. It also wasn't lost on me that these intense workouts were killing my addictive drug cravings…big time. The workouts were full-tilt and showing up with a hangover, or worse, was a sure way to end up puking out back in the alley.

After acclimating to the heat, I kind of liked the routine. It was broken into three segments. The first 20 minutes was all about conditioning and strength. It was as good as any physical workout I'd ever participated in. There were no breaks between procedures. There was no cheating or cutting corners because everyone was there to better themselves. All the students, regardless of rank, pushed themselves to their own personal limits and abilities.

Mr. Lilly paced us alternately with shouting and then gentle persuasion. One thing that immediately impressed me was that when he asked us to do a particularly difficult exercise, he would do two of them himself.

The next obvious thing to me was that every student endeavored to do their best, not only for their own benefit, but because they respected and admired the *Sabum*.

Mr. Lilly himself was an enigma. He was a Conch, born and raised in Key West, but was also an *old soul*. He didn't drive a car and rode his bike to the dojang. He had no telephone at home, although there was one at the school. He was definitely *old school*. He didn't go out much or frequent bars. When I asked him why, he'd say, "I used to be a brawler, and there's too many drunks out there that are beggin' for a beat-down." Taekwondo had given him a satisfying discipline, and the lure of street brawling had brought him nothing but trouble. In martial arts there was honor. There was a comforting feeling in knowing that if you had the skill to overpower someone, you no longer had the need to prove it. Martial arts was not only a way to fight…but a way to live.

I was quickly realizing the depth of not only Mr. Lilly's commitment, but the commitment of his students.

The second segment of class was dedicated to martial arts techniques. The art of Taekwondo is 80-to-90 percent kicking: front kicks, side kicks, back kicks, round kicks, spin kicks, jump kicks, etc.,…you get the idea.

Ten repetitions of each particular kick with both legs, and a few punches thrown in while counting in Korean, can fill that second 20 minutes pretty fast.

After a two-minute rest to catch our breath, the remaining time was spent on forms.

Each form features a focus on an individual move and, when tested, represents a different colored belt level. Every Friday class was *OPEN SPARRING*. That was the most fun because it allowed everyone to find out how things really worked, or not.

In the ATA belt system there are eight colors before reaching Black Belt. They use the metaphor of the growth of a pine tree to signify the different belt levels. Each rank has basic movement, footwork, sparring combos and self-defense,

The first belt is *WHITE* and is assigned to all beginners. White embodies innocence, as that of the of the new student.

ORANGE is the rising sun bringing growing energy to the new planted seed.

YELLOW are the seeds from which the pine tree sprouts.

GREEN is the plant's growth, as Taekwondo skills begin to develop.

BLUE is the heaven, towards which the plant grows into a tree.

PURPLE belt marks the beginning of a deeper appreciation of what the black belt means. It is the color that the sky takes on right before the dawn.

BROWN represents the ripening of the tree as the advanced student begins to mature.

RED indicates a more detailed knowledge and mastery of TaeKwonDo, but also serves as a warning. DANGER! This student now has power, technique and knowledge but must now perfect his/her control. At this stage, Mr. Lilly would have us perform a full-power kick to an opponent that would contact (and pop) his uniform, but would NOT touch his body. That test exhibited the laser sharp control that was required for Black Belt advancement. VOLUNTEERING to be the dummy was MANDATORY.

Advancement testing was offered every 2-4 months and the average time from white to black belt was generally in the 3-4 year range if you attended 3-4 classes per week.

It was exhausting. It was painful, and it was demanding, but advancement was incredibly satisfying. The tests were usually broken down into form/technique, sparring, and power demonstrations, for example, board breaking, etc.

BLACK BELT symbolizes responsibility, perseverance and self-discipline. It is the ultimate degree of years of sacrifice and personal aspiration. Although it is a ceiling for some, it is also the beginning of advanced techniques, or succeeding levels of *BLACK BELT.*

5th Degree Dan (Black) indicates a MASTER. As I studied with Mr. Lilly, he was 4th degree Black and working toward MASTER. It takes many years but, as any advanced martial artist will tell you, *The JOURNEY is the THING.*

We actually had homework, such as learning words and phrases in Korean and studying Korean history. As I was observing all this, one of my most meaningful martial arts experiences was about to evolve.

I had just advanced to Green Belt when I came to class one afternoon, excited to begin working on a new form. As I entered and bowed, I noticed Mr. Lilly putting a poster up on the dojang wall. It was for the Taekwondo National Championships, to be held in Orlando in the winter of 1994.

I read the poster and exclaimed: "Wow, I'm working a juggling gig for a convention in Orlando that same weekend. Maybe I'll get over there and watch some of it."

Mr. Lilly, with his usual deadpan expression, said: "If you're going to be there that week-end, you should sign up and compete."

Hahaha. I had a good laugh and said, "I'm not sure I'm ready to go that far, but thanks for the compliment." Then I took my shoes off and prepared for class.

We commenced with our usual regimen of stretching and calisthenics. Suddenly Mr. Lilly asked everyone to stand at attention, and then directed them to turn to me.

"I want everyone to wish Mr. Soto good luck," he said. "He's going to compete in the TaeKwonDo Winternationals in Orlando next month!"

HOLY CRAP!!!

I wasn't sure if I was being punked or promoted. I don't blush easily…but I must've turned beet red. The rest of the class was a blur to me. My mind raced. How embarrassing. Not only was I set up to be a lowly Green Belt punching bag at a tournament, but then I'd have to come back to my own dojang as a possible failure.

150

But there was no alternative. After that announcement by my Sabum, I knew that no excuse for skipping the contest would ever allow me to look Mr. Lilly, or my fellow students, in the eyes again.

After class, as everyone wished me good luck, I tried to cop a lame plea to Mr. Lilly, but he was ready for me.

"Don't worry Mr. Soto," he preempted. "They break everyone down into relevant categories by sex, age and belt level. You'll only be competing against people of your own level, and it'll be a great experience for you."

I went home and felt like crawling in a hole and hiding. I never in a million years felt like I was ready for a competition, let alone on the national level.

Now I was on the clock. I only had about six or seven weeks to train and knew that if I didn't want be the punch line (pun intended) of a joke, then I'd better focus like never before.

The time, of course, flew by as the tournament date approached. I resigned myself to just doing the best I could and to live with the results.

And now it was SHOWTIME.

Orlando here I come.

After finishing my convention performance gig on Friday night at the Dolphin Hotel, one of the Walt Disney World Resorts, I went back to my room, showered and tried to get some sleep. Fat chance!

Registration for the tournament was at 9am at

the Marriott Convention Center, near Universal Studios.

I got up early, had my morning *Cafe con Leche* (Cuban rocket fuel) and took a walk. Then I stretched and practiced my form. Mr. Lilly had explained to me that the competition was divided into *FORMS* and *SPARRING*.

When I arrived at the Marriott tournament site, there were crowds of martial artists unloading their gear in the parking lot. Each contestant had their individual school/dojang logo patches displayed prominently on their dobuks.

Holy Frijoles! It was buzzing like a beehive. A veritable sea of anxious contestants...all in white.

I gathered my dobuk and sparring gear and sought out the changing room and the registration desk.

The two major impressions I had immediately was 1) that each school had four to six entrants, and 2) EVERYONE, from 7-70 years old and white to black belts, was exceedingly friendly and helpful. It's a good thing too, because I was alone and intimidated.

No matter. I was greeted like family. Everyone was polite, helpful and respectful. NOT ONE SINGLE BAD ATTITUDE.

How refreshing I thought. These people are all here to fight each other but it feels more like a family reunion. Everyone was introducing themselves, shaking hands and bowing. It was then that I realized what Mr. Lilly meant when he said, "It'll be a great experience for you."

All these contestants, having successfully triumphed over anger and emotion, were now enjoying this challenge as a sport. The giant convention hall was filled with hundreds of contenders. There were competition rings taped out on the floor and the PA system would direct you to your particular location. The helpful volunteers directed me to my venue.

I watched several bouts and took mental notes. Then…it was NOW.

ALL GEEN BELT MEN, AGES 35-50, PLEASE REPORT TO RING BRAVO!

I'd like to go into detail about my performances and round-robin competitions but I was so nervous that it seemed like a dream-state. The sparring scores were tabulated by a point system, and the forms were judged by technique.

Each time my name was called I breathed deep, focused and just gave it my best shot.

Afterward I was in complete awe that everyone there who had come to fight and compete with each other were bowing and even hugging after intense matches. It wasn't scary or threatening like I imagined it might have been, but proud and honorable. Again I heard the echo of *"It'll be a great experience for you."*

When I finished I felt such a sense of elation. Soaking wet with sweat, I knelt down and enjoyed watching and learning while the Black Belts, the last group to go, did their thing. It was an exciting finale.

Then, as the Grand Master thanked everyone for a successful tournament, they began to call the different belt level winners to the stage.

I was so thankful that Mr. Lilly had "tricked" me into this "experience," when suddenly…they announced my name. "THIRD PLACE in both sparring and form in Green Belt…WILL SOTO from Key West Martial Arts."

Shocked…would be an understatement. I rose and joined the other trophy winners onstage to the roar in the auditorium. I was numb. I was as stunned as I was proud.

When the presentations were done, I gathered my gear and said goodbye and thank you to anyone who would listen. I walked out to my truck, threw my stuff in the back and plopped in.

Then it all hit me…like a ton of bricks. Almost a year before I had been struggling with drug dependence. My fear and shame from those days were a distant, but still distinct, memory.

I looked down at my trophies and thought of Mr. Lilly and my supportive fellow students…and just burst into tears. I literally sobbed like a baby for a good five to ten minutes. It was a cleansing cry. Not because I had been successful, but because I was finally healthy again.

I had found that good habit to replace the bad one.

When I returned home I was a new person…or at least the old one that I once loved being. I had regained my self-confidence, my self-respect and re-felt the mojo that once was my trademark.

It was in the midst of this renaissance when I

met Amy. We knew that we were soul-mates immediately and, as we now move toward 25 years together, I know that my training and renewed health focus were major factors in making our relationship a possibility.

I continued to study under Mr. Lilly's guidance for several more years until finally Mr. Malpica and I received our Black Belts in a ceremony at the TOP, a convention room at the La Concha Hotel. It was one of the proudest moments of my life, and Amy was there to share it with me.

In the tradition of many Black Belts, I went on to continuing education, teaching and training other students in the ancient style that was so important to me. I continued to compete by traveling to other tournaments with Mr. Malpica. He actually went on to become a World Champion 1st degree Black Belt and I also gathered a few more trophies, but none ever more meaningful to me than that first "experience" in Orlando.

I sometimes like to say that Mr. Lilly helped *save my life,* but the truth is he just opened the door to salvation…and coaxed me through it.

He is gone now, is in heaven, but will live in my heart forever.

As I write this, my Black Belt, along with its certificate and a picture of Mr. Lilly, Mr. Malpica and myself hang on the wall just above my computer.

Thank you **Mr. Robert Ward Lilly**. Rest in Peace my Brother and Sabum. I will never forget you.

KAHM SAHM NEE-DA

AFTERWORD

Why a book?

I decided to share these experiences with you for one special reason. Key West, the only place that I have ever lovingly called home, is a catalyst for magic.

It's a special place that can't be easily described as a tropical island, a Florida city, or a vacation destination.

I believe there are some mystic forces at work here. Granted, these forces do not seem to affect every person. I know more than one person who has come here and left because they hadn't felt the magnetism of which I write. It's true, Key West is not for everyone. The eccentric little island does have its warts and challenges, but for those of us who've fallen prey to the allure and mystical charm of this little ocean outpost, the presence of a greater power is unexplainable.

There are just too many occurrences and coincidences here, that defy logic or normalcy, to go unnoticed.

Some of the tales I've related here are heartwarming, some are humorous, some are frightening and some just notable, but all of them seem to reflect the Florida Keys tourism motto…

"CLOSE TO PERFECT, FAR FROM NORMAL."

Again, these stories are not really about me, my strengths or my weaknesses. They're about the aura of a place that seems to transcend rationale on a regular basis. I really believe that these revelations of joy, love, fear and personal tribulations are unique and deserve to be shared, whether or not they are understood. It's not just the climate, or the people or the remoteness of an island at the end of the Florida Keys, although these factors all play a part. It's more about a feeling, a connection and a magic that I, and many others, found quite by accident.

Several of these sagas have occurred outside the boundaries of Key West, but would not have been possible without the Keys' influence. The most significant thread of familiarity in all of this, I believe, is the people.

The *Conchs*, as Keys residents are fondly referred to, are a unique bunch of loving survivalists, who humorously have no particular use for logic, rules or the rest of Florida. Outsiders that live more than seven years in the Keys are considered *FRESH-WATER CONCHS*. That being said, if you love folks here…they love you back. They don't care what your past history or financial status is. If your word is good then that's all they need. After 43 years here I'm proud to have been awarded HONORARY

CONCH status by Kermit Lewin, then Mayor of Monroe County, but it's not the certificate, but the community love and acceptance that I cherish the most.

It's said that there is the family you're given at birth…and the family that you choose. I'm forever grateful to my *Conch* family. My favorite coined phrase here, sometimes credited to Steven Tyler, is *"We're all here, because we're not all there."*

When I first came to Key West as a civilian, the first notable character I met ended up being my mentor for the next 30 years. Captain Tony Tarracino. He, and my father, Will, were the two most influential men in my life. They both guided me to *FOLLOW YOUR HEART* and *CHERISH YOUR FRIENDS*.

My mom, Elaine, who was my biggest fan, always reminded me that that life was short, and to live your life doing the things that make you happy and whole is the biggest success of all. What could possibly be more fulfilling than doing what you love, with the people who inspire you and in the place that makes you happy.

I dedicate this book to all three of them and to my wife, Amy Meshew-Soto, my soul-mate and the light of my life. We complete each other like no other relationship I've ever experienced. We are One.

My second tier of Thank Yous goes to those friends and supporters, without whose help this book, and my magical life in Key West, wouldn't have had such a happy outcome.

My intrepid writing mentors, Jon and Gabrielle Breakfield, although a continent away, were never further than my MAC desktop. They were there at any hour of the day or night, serving as my coaches, editors, technical advisers and friends. Their advice was inspirational, truthful, encouraging and brutally honest...all the things a novice author really needs.

I've wanted to write for some time, but just couldn't put all the required pieces together. Sort of like having a car and a destination, but not knowing how to drive or find directions. Jon and Gabrielle have been my GPS. Now I'm buzzing along, full of excitement about my new journey.

Thanks to them for showing me the route and how to stay on the road. I can honestly say that without their dedication, there would be no book. They're now officially part of the family I *CHOSE*. They've gone far beyond the call of duty.

Others that deserve special thanks are the true-blue friends that were always there for me, whether I was on top of the world or off-the-rails. They include...

Kevin and Robin Beede,
Bill and Kathy Kight,
Richard and Karen Bertocci,
Ben and Valerie Waggoner,
Phil and Lane Everett,
Richard and Kelly Klitenick,
Clark and June Luster,
Patti Fernandez (sailing friend and adviser),
John Taheny (my best friend and expert High-

wire rigger),

Danny Keith Reed (my Key West rig/set-up man for 20 years),

Mike Mongo (my bud, computer techie and astronaut teacher),

Pete Lazaro (my sailing companion and Brother), and my sibs, Robert, Patt and Donna.

Beyond that, I thank the entire community of Key West, whose official motto, *ONE HUMAN FAMILY,* says it all.

I intend to honor all of them by paying it forward.

To you readers, thank you for sharing your time with me. As a performer, I'll always be grateful to my fans, friends and audience that cheer me on to *Push the Package* in my public shows. Now, as a neophyte author, I can share some of my more intimate experiences of a place that stole my heart and still thrills my soul.

Now that I'm rolling…I look forward to seeing you again in Volume #2 of Key West Rogue Diaries.

I'm wishing everyone gorgeous sunsets and happy fantasies…

…until we meet again.

Made in the USA
Monee, IL
15 May 2021